HIKES LIST

MENASHA RIDGE PRESS
Birmingham, Alabama

60 HIKES WITHIN 60 MILES

SAN ANTONIO & AUSTIN

INCLUDING THE HILL COUNTRY

SECOND EDITION

TOM TAYLOR

AND

JOHNNY MOLLOY

DISCLAIMER

This book is meant only as a guide to select trails in the San Antonio and Austin areas and does not guarantee hiker safety in any way—you hike at your own risk. Neither Menasha Ridge Press, Tom Taylor, nor Johnny Molloy is liable for property loss or damage, personal injury, or death that result in any way from accessing or hiking the trails described in the following pages. Please be aware that hikers have been injured in the San Antonio and Austin areas. Be especially cautious when walking on or near boulders, steep inclines, and drop-offs, and do not attempt to explore terrain that may be beyond your abilities. To help ensure an uneventful hike, please read carefully the introduction to this book, and perhaps get further safety information and guidance from other sources. Familiarize yourself thoroughly with the areas you intend to visit before venturing out. Ask questions, and prepare for the unforeseen. Familiarize yourself with current weather reports, maps of the area you intend to visit, and any relevant park regulations.

Copyright © 2008 Tom Taylor and Johnny Molloy
All rights reserved
Printed in the United States of America
Published by Menasha Ridge Press
Distributed by Publishers Group West
Second edition, fourth printing 2009

Library of Congress Cataloging-in-Publication Data
    Taylor, Tom, 1970–
        60 hikes within 60 miles, San Antonio & Austin, including the hill
        country/Tom Taylor and Johnny Molloy.—2nd ed.
    p. cm.
    Includes index.
    ISBN-13: 978-0-89732-533-2
    ISBN-10: 0-89732-533-8
        1. Hiking—Texas—San Antonio Region—Guidebooks. 2. Hiking—
    Texas—Austin Region—Guidebooks. 3. Trails—Texas—San Antonio
    Region—Guidebooks. 4. Trails—Texas—Austin Region—Guidebooks.
    5. San Antonio Region (Tex.)—Guidebooks. 6. Austin Region (Tex.)—
    Guidebooks. I. Title: Sixty hikes within sixty miles, San Antonio and
    Austin, including the hill country. II. Molloy, Johnny, 1961– III. Title.

GV199.42.T492S368 2008
796.5209764'351—dc22

                                    2007026677

Cover and text design by Steveco International
Cover photo copyright © Johnny Molloy
Johnny Molloy photo (page ix) by Lynette Barker
All other photos by Johnny Molloy
Maps by Steve Jones and Scott McGrew

Menasha Ridge Press
P.O. Box 43673
Birmingham, AL 35243
www.menasharidge.com

FOR MY WIFE AND TRAIL PARTNER, DALE. — TOM TAYLOR
FOR ALL THE HIKERS IN THE LONE STAR STATE. — JOHNNY MOLLOY

TABLE OF CONTENTS

ACKNOWLEDGMENTS

A lot of people helped to make this book possible, many of them unaware of it, including the staff at all of the parks and preserves who provided directions, insight, and advice about the areas they care for on a daily basis. I could never have found all of the hiking gems that I did without their guidance and enthusiasm.

On an individual level, this guide wouldn't have seen completion without the guidance of Bud Zehmer and Russell Helms, and especially my coauthor, Johnny Molloy. It wouldn't have been written without them. I'm deeply indebted.

—TOM TAYLOR

Thanks to all the folks at the Environmental Education Center at McKinney Roughs, Jennifer McCoy, Betsey Terrell, Helen and her children and sister in southern Mexico, Scott Taylor at Landa Park, and Agdel Rivera at San Antonio Parks and Recreation Department. Thanks to Eric Salys for going hiking with me and advising me about all sorts of stuff, even at the expense of his car window.

—JOHNNY MOLLOY

FOREWORD

Welcome to Menasha Ridge Press's *60 Hikes within 60 Miles*. Our strategy was simple: First, find a hiker who knows the area and loves to hike. Second, ask that person to spend a year researching the most popular and very best trails around. And third, have that person describe each trail in terms of difficulty, scenery, condition, elevation change, and all other categories of information that are important to hikers. "Pretend you've just completed a hike and met up with other hikers at the trailhead," we told each author. "Imagine their questions, and be clear in your answers." Experienced hikers and writer, authors Johnny Molloy and Tom Taylor have selected 60 of the best hikes in and around the San Antonio and Austin areas. From urban hikes that make use of parklands to aerobic outings in national forests, Molloy and Taylor provide hikers (and walkers) with a great variety of hikes—and all within roughly 60 miles of San Antonio and Austin.

You'll get more out of this book if you take a moment to read the Introduction explaining how to read the trail listings. The "Topographic Maps" section will help you understand how useful topos will be on a hike, and will also tell you where to get them. And though this is a "where-to" rather than a "how-to" guide, those of you who have hiked extensively will find the Introduction of particular value. As much for the opportunity to free the spirit as well as to free the body, let these hikes elevate you above the urban hurry.

All the best,
The Editors at Menasha Ridge Press

ABOUT THE AUTHORS

JOHNNY MOLLOY is an outdoor writer based in Johnson City, Tennessee. Born in Memphis, he moved to Knoxville in 1980 to attend the University of Tennessee. During his college years, he developed a love of the natural world that has become the primary focus his life.

It all started on a backpacking foray into Great Smoky Mountains National Park. That first trip was a disaster; nevertheless, Johnny discovered a love of the outdoors that would lead him to canoe-camp and backpack throughout the United States and abroad over the next 25 years. Today, he averages 150 nights out per year.

After graduating from UT in 1987 with a degree in economics, Johnny spent an ever-increasing amount of time in the wild, becoming more skilled in a variety of environments. Friends enjoyed his adventure stories; one even suggested he write a book. He pursued that idea and soon parlayed his love of the outdoors into an occupation.

The results of his efforts are more than 30 books, including hiking, camping, paddling, and other comprehensive guidebooks, as well as books on true outdoor adventures. He has also written numerous articles for magazines and Web sites, and he continues to write and travel extensively to all four corners of the United States, endeavoring in a variety of outdoor pursuits. For the latest on Johnny, visit his Web site, **www.johnnymolloy.com**.

Whether tracking game, looking for a secluded fishing spot, or just wandering the countryside, **TOM TAYLOR** spends a great deal of time on Texas's trails. A native raised in west Texas, he migrated to the Hill Country area to take advantage of all it has to offer in outdoor recreation. Tom now resides in San Antonio.

PREFACE

I'm not one who walks for the sake of walking. Exercise isn't a good enough excuse. However, I'll walk for miles to see something out of the ordinary, or extremely beautiful. I also love to hike just to get away from it all. I think the hikes in this book reflect this. My hope is that you'll enjoy these hikes, and find them to be just as interesting as I did.

There are a lot of curious things to see out on these trails. Some of the sites are inspiring, and some of them are just plain curious. Not the type of thing you see every day, if you will. In Palmetto State Park, there is an old wagon wheel with a tree that has grown right through it. Both the wheel and the tree have been around much longer than any of us. This is downright interesting to me. In fact, I'm still trying to figure out what happened.

Sometimes, just the opportunity to see something interesting is enough. The blinds overlooking the Colorado River at Hornsby Bend offer the possibility of some great bird viewing, as well as other small wildlife. At the right time of year, you could sit all day in the cool fall air and watch the migrating ducks as they make their way through the central flyway. This is worth the trip, and it's a healthy hike to boot. Not too challenging, and definitely not what you'd expect to find near a water treatment facility. Yet there it is. Interesting.

If you follow the Twin Peaks hike to its apex, you'll stand your best chance in this part of the country of seeing a mountain lion. They are out there, but you'll have to sit still to catch one in the distance. This won't be a problem, because by the time you reach the peak you'll be ready to rest a bit. Just keep your eyes open.

All of the trails, even the ones in the middle of San Antonio or Austin, contain a wide variety of wildlife, if you just look. McAllister Park, one of the busiest, and located in San Antonio, has one of the largest deer populations of any of the hikes in this book. It's also where I saw the most snakes, by the way. If you look hard enough, and are quiet enough, you could see deer at every park and preserve in this book. You'll also find abundant and diverse species of birds.

Texas plays host to more than 600 species of birds. Being located in the South Central part of the state, near the woods and the coast, allows you to see a lot of them right here. There are rare painted buntings at McKinney Falls on the Homestead Trail, a large variety of sparrows and finches everywhere, and cardinals, jays, titmice, and more to be seen on these trails. I've spotted a pileated woodpecker in Buescher State Park. Very rare for these parts. To enrich your bird-watching, pick up a bird guide before you go hiking. I never leave home without my binoculars and bird guide.

Keep your eyes on the ground and you could see everything from coral snakes to the rare Houston toad. Big tarantulas (especially in Buescher) live deeper in the woods, too. One of the most fascinating trails for local wildlife is in Lockhart State Park. Huge garden spiders build webs more than ten feet wide across the trails. You can't miss them, so don't walk into them. Although toads and spiders are creepy to some, these kinds of encounters are worth the drive for me.

While I was hiking these trails I discovered a new hobby, geocaching, that has really taken hold in our area. For those not familiar with it, geocaching is a high-tech scavenger hunt that is an outgrowth of an older sport known as letter boxing. Participants hide and look for "treasures" in out-of-the-way locations based solely on GPS coordinates and cryptic clues. It can certainly make a trail just that much more interesting, and you should learn more about it. For more information, **www.geocaching.com** is worth checking out. There you'll be able to learn about caches located in the San Antonio and Austin area. A lot of people have gone to a lot of trouble to help this activity catch on. It's a rapidly growing community around here.

And the community on the trails around here is sizable. A lot of hikers in the area make regular use of our extensive range of trails and tend to take good care of them, too. Some of the most beautiful trails, and some that would seem more out of the way, see a lot of traffic on weekends. For a better chance at solitude, any of your trips would benefit from going during the week rather than the weekend.

However, at some parks crowding doesn't seem to be related to the time of day or year. McAllister Park is always busy. All day, every day, all year long. The Hill Country SNA sees an awful lot of traffic for its remote location as well. If you're looking for a rugged hike, it's your place, but if you're looking for solitude, it might not be for you. This leads me to my favorite hike of all those in the book . . . .

Friedrich Wilderness Park. This trail is located close to San Antonio, and is very unique among most trails in our area. It offers a lot of elevation change, and seems to have more in common with the mountain states than with Texas. It is very secluded, and sees little use. After you've hiked—and climbed—to the stone fence halfway through, and realize you haven't seen anyone else, it'll set in. Just sit on the fence and listen to the silence. It's a great trail, my personal favorite.

All of the parks and trails, however, are worth visiting and, more so, worth preserving. If you get a chance to contribute to a donation box for maintenance, please do so, especially if you enjoyed the trail. Every trail in this book is worth a few dollars to visit.

—TOM TAYLOR

RECOMMENDED HIKES

HIKES FROM 1 TO 3 MILES

HIKES FROM 3 TO 6 MILES

HIKES MORE THAN 6 MILES

HIKES GOOD FOR YOUNG CHILDREN

SCENIC HIKES (continued)

HISTORIC HIKES

HIKES FOR WILDLIFE VIEWING

HIKES FOR WILDFLOWERS

TRAILS FOR BICYCLISTS

TRAILS FOR RUNNERS

LESS-BUSY HIKES

LESS-BUSY HIKES (continued)

HEAVILY TRAVELED HIKES

INTRODUCTION

Welcome to *60 Hikes within 60 Miles: San Antonio & Austin*! If you're new to hiking or even if you're a seasoned trailsmith, take a few minutes to read the following introduction. We explain how this book is organized and how to use it.

HIKE DESCRIPTIONS

Each hike contains six key items: a locator map, an In Brief description of the trail, an At-a-Glance Information box, directions to the trail, a trail map, and a hike narrative. Combined, the maps and information provide a clear method to assess each trail from the comfort of your home.

LOCATOR MAP

After narrowing down the general area of the hike on the overview map, the locator map, along with driving directions given in the narrative, enables you to find the trailhead. Once at the trailheads, park only in designated areas.

IN BRIEF

This synopsis of the trail offers a snapshot of what to expect along the trail, including mention of any historical sights, beautiful vistas, or other interesting sights you may encounter.

AT-A-GLANCE INFORMATION

The At-a-Glance boxes give you a quick idea of the specifics of each hike. Twelve basic elements are covered:

LENGTH The length of the trail from start to finish. There may be options to shorten or extend the hikes, but the mileage corresponds to the described hike. Consult the hike description to help decide how to customize the hike for your ability or time constraints.

CONFIGURATION A description of what the trail might look like from overhead. Trails can be loops, out-and-backs (that is, along the same route), figure eights, or balloons. Sometimes the descriptions might surprise you.

DIFFICULTY The degree of effort an "average" hiker should expect on a given hike. For simplicity, difficulty is described as "easy," "moderate," or "difficult."

SCENERY Rates the overall environs of the hike and what to expect in terms of plant life, wildlife, streams, or historic buildings.

EXPOSURE A quick check of how much sun you can expect on your shoulders during the hike. Descriptors used are self-explanatory and include terms such as "shady," "exposed," and "sunny."

SOLITUDE Indicates how busy the trail might be on an average day. Trail traffic, of course, will vary from day to day and season to season.

TRAIL SURFACE Indicates whether the trail is paved, rocky, smooth dirt, or a mixture of elements.

HIKING TIME How long it took the author to hike the trail. Hiking times include the occasional stop to "smell the roses" or to take in a nice view.

ACCESS Notes fees or permits needed to access the trail. In most cases no fees or permits are required. Always check if in doubt.

MAPS Which map is the best, in the author's opinion, for this hike and where you get it.

FACILITIES Notes any facilities such as restrooms, phones, and water available at the trailhead or on the trail.

SPECIAL COMMENTS Provides you with those little extra details that don't fit into any of the above categories. Here you'll find information on trail hiking options and facts such as whether or not to expect to a lifeguard at a nearby swimming beach.

DIRECTIONS

Check here for directions to the trailhead. Used with the locator map, the directions will help you locate each trailhead.

DESCRIPTIONS

The trail description is the heart of each hike. Here, the author provides a summary of the trail's essence and highlights any special traits that the hike offers. Ultimately the hike description will help you choose which hikes are best for you.

NEARBY ACTIVITIES

Not every hike will have this listing. For those that do, look here for information on nearby dining opportunities or other activities to fill out your day.

WEATHER

With the exception of July, August, and September, the weather for hiking in the Hill Country can be great. Even the summer months have cool mornings that you can take advantage of. The best times are October and November and March through May. Depending on the severity of winter, December can be just as pleasant as early fall. The main things to watch out for are the heat, which can be brutal in the summer, and the rains. With all the rivers in the area, flash floods can be a real problem for unwary hikers. The Guadalupe River, for example, has flooded to the point of washing homes away twice in less than ten years, and it doesn't take long for the waters to reach dangerous levels. What might seem like a pleasant light rain for a hike could turn to disaster. With the heat, hydration is key. Carry lots of water, and get off the trails before morning is gone.

Average Daily Temperatures by Month: San Antonio and Austin

	Jan	Feb	Mar	Apr	May	Jun
High	59°F	63°F	72°F	79°F	85°F	91°F
Low	39°F	42°F	51°F	60°F	67°F	71°F

	Jul	Aug	Sep	Oct	Nov	Dec
High	95°F	96°F	90°F	82°F	72°F	62°F
Low	74°F	74°F	70°F	60°F	50°F	41°F

MAPS

The maps in this book have been produced with great care and, used with the hiking directions, will help you stay on course. But as any experienced hiker knows, things can get tricky off the beaten path.

The maps in this book, when used with the route directions present in each chapter, are sufficient to direct you to the trail and guide you on it. However, you will find superior detail and valuable information in the United States Geological Survey's 7.5-minute series topographic maps. Topo maps are available online in many locations. The easiest single Web resource is located at **terraserver .microsoft.com.** You can view and print topos of the entire Unites States there, and view aerial photographs of the entire Unites States, as well. The downside to topos is that most of them are outdated, having been created 20 to 30 years ago. But they still provide excellent topographic detail.

If you're new to hiking you might be wondering, "What's a topographic map?"

In short, a topo indicates not only linear distance but elevation as well, using contour lines. Wavy contour lines spread across topo maps, each line representing a particular elevation. At the base of each topo, a contour's interval designation is given.

If the contour interval is 200 feet, then the distance between each contour line is 200 feet. Follow five contour lines up on a map and the elevation has increased by 1,000 feet.

In addition to outdoor shops and bike shops, you'll find topos at major universities and some public libraries, where you might try photocopying the ones you need to avoid the cost of buying them. But if you want your own and can't find them locally, contact the United States Geological Survey at (888) ASK-USGS or visit **www.usgs.gov.**

TRAIL ETIQUETTE

Whether you're on a city, county, state, or national park trail, always remember that great care and resources (from nature as well as from your tax dollars) have gone into creating these trails. Treat the trail, wildlife, and fellow hikers with respect.

1. **Hike on open trails only. Respect trail and road closures (ask if not sure), avoid possibly trespassing on private land, and obtain permits and authorization as required. Leave gates as you found them or as marked.**

2. **Leave no trace of your visit other than footprints. Be sensitive to the ground beneath you. This also means staying on the trail and not creating any new ones. Be sure to pack out what you pack in. No one likes to see the trash someone else has left behind.**

3. **Never spook animals. An unannounced approach, a sudden movement, or a loud noise startles all animals. This can be dangerous for you, for others, and for the animals. Give animals extra room and time to adjust to you.**

4. **Plan ahead. Know your equipment, your ability, and the area in which you are hiking—and prepare accordingly. Be self-sufficient at all times; carry necessary supplies for changes in weather or other conditions. A well-executed trip is a satisfaction to you and not a burden to others.**

5. **Be courteous to other hikers or bikers you meet on the trails.**

WATER

"How much is enough? One bottle? Two? Three? But think of all that extra weight!" Well, one simple physiological fact should convince you to err on the side of excess when it comes to deciding how much water to pack: a hiker working hard in 90-degree heat needs approximately ten quarts of fluid every day. That's two and a half gallons—12 large water bottles or 16 small ones. In other words, pack along one or two bottles even for short hikes.

Serious backpackers hit the trail prepared to purify water found along the route. This method, while less dangerous than drinking it untreated, comes with risks. Purifiers with ceramic filters are the safest, but are also the most expensive. Many hikers pack along the slightly distasteful tetraglycine hydroperiodide tablets (sold under the names Potable Aqua, Coughlan's, and others).

Probably the most common water-borne "bug" that hikers face is giardia, which may not hit until one to four weeks after ingestion. It will have you passing noxious rotten-egg gas, vomiting, shivering with chills, and living in the bathroom. But there are other parasites to worry about, including E. coli and cryptosporidium (that are harder to kill than giardia).

For most people, the pleasures of hiking make carrying water a relatively minor price to pay to remain healthy. If you're tempted to drink "found water," do so only if you understand the risks involved. Better yet, hydrate prior to your hike, carry (and drink) six ounces of water for every mile you plan to hike, and hydrate after the hike.

FIRST-AID KIT

A typical kit may contain more items than you might think necessary. But these are just the basics. Pack the items in a waterproof bag such as a Ziploc bag or a similar product.

Ace bandages or Spenco joint wraps

Antibiotic ointment (Neosporin or the generic equivalent)

Aspirin, ibuprofen, or acetaminophen

Band-Aids

Benadryl or the generic equivalent, diphenhydramine (in case of allergic reactions)

Butterfly-closure bandages

Epinephrine in a prefilled syringe (for people known to have severe allergic reactions to such things as bee stings)

Gauze (one roll)

Gauze compress pads (a half-dozen 4- x 4-inch pads)

Hydrogen peroxide, Betadine, or iodine

Insect repellent

Matches or pocket lighter

Moleskin/Spenco "Second Skin"

Sunscreen

Whistle (it's more effective in signaling rescuers than your voice)

HIKING WITH CHILDREN

No one is ever too young for a nice hike in the woods or through a city park. Parents with infants can strap on little ones with the popular Snugli device. Be careful, though. Flat, short trails are probably best with an infant. Toddlers who have not quite mastered walking can still tag along, riding on an adult's back in a child carrier

Children who are walking can, of course, follow along with an adult. Use common sense to judge a child's capacity to hike a particular trail. Always rely on the possibility that the child will tire quickly and have to be carried.

When packing for the hike, remember the needs of the child as well as your own. Make sure children are adequately clothed for the weather, have proper shoes, and are properly protected from the sun with sunscreen and clothing. Kids can dehydrate quickly, so make sure you have plenty of fluid for everyone.

Depending on age, ability, and the hike's length and difficulty, most children should enjoy the shorter hikes described in this book. To assist an adult with determining which trails are suitable for children, a list of hike recommendations for children is provided on page xiv.

THE BUSINESS HIKER

Whether in the San Antonio–Austin area on business, as a resident, or as a visitor, you'll find many quick getaways perfect for a long lunch escape or an evening hike to unwind from a busy day at the office or convention. Instead of staying cooped up inside, head out to one of the many parks and conservation areas on the fringes of the metro area and combine lunch with a relaxing walk.

TICKS

Ticks like to hang out in the brush that grows along trails. July is a peak month for ticks, but you should be tick-aware during all months of the spring, summer, and fall. Ticks, actually arthropods and not insects, are ectoparasites, which need a host for the majority of their life cycle in order to reproduce. The ticks that light onto you while hiking will be very small, sometimes so tiny that you won't be able to spot them. Primarily of two varieties, deer ticks and dog ticks, both need a few hours of actual attachment before they can transmit any disease they may harbor. I've found ticks in my socks and on my legs several hours after a hike that have not yet anchored. The best strategy is to visually check every half-hour or so while hiking, do a thorough check before you get in the car, and then, when you take a posthike shower, do an even more thorough check of your entire body. Ticks that haven't latched on are easily removed, but not easily killed. If I pick off a tick in the woods, I just toss it aside. If I find one on my person at home, I make sure to dispatch it down the toilet. For ticks that have embedded, removal with tweezers is best.

POISON IVY, OAK, AND SUMAC

Recognizing and avoiding contact with poison ivy, oak, and sumac is the most effective way to prevent the painful, itchy rashes associated with these plants. Poison ivy occurs as a vine or shrub, with three leaflets to a leaf; poison oak occurs as either a vine or shrub, with three leaflets as well; and poison sumac flourishes in swampland, with each leaf containing 7 to 13 leaflets. Urushiol, the oil in the sap of these plants, is responsible for the rash.

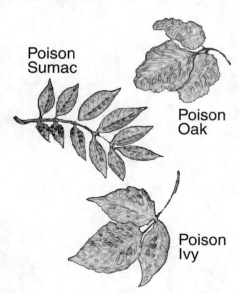

Within 12 to 24 hours of exposure, raised lines and/or blisters will appear, accompanied by a terrible itch. Refrain from scratching because bacteria under fingernails may cause infection. Wash and dry the rash thoroughly, applying a calamine lotion to help dry out the rash. If itching or blistering is severe, seek medical attention. If you do come into contact with one of these plants, remember that oil-contaminated clothes, pets, or hiking gear can easily inflict an irritating rash on you or someone else, so wash not only any exposed parts of your body but also clothes, gear, and pets, if applicable.

AUSTIN

01 BULL CREEK TRAIL

KEY AT-A-GLANCE INFORMATION

LENGTH: 4 miles

CONFIGURATION: Out-and-back

DIFFICULTY: Easy

SCENERY: Riparian woodland and water

EXPOSURE: Mostly shady

TRAFFIC: Light

TRAIL SURFACE: Dirt

HIKING TIME: 2.5 hours

ACCESS: Open to the public 5 a.m.–10 p.m.

MAPS: Available online at www.bullcreek.net

FACILITIES: Restrooms at both ends of trail

IN BRIEF

This secluded area of south Austin is conspicuously located right under one of its busiest roads. An array of birds and creek dwellers await informed hikers.

DESCRIPTION

The park in which this hike starts is in a familiar area. A small parking lot, restrooms, and a couple of picnic tables stand silently in this quiet little area. The creek forms a pool suitable for swimming in the park area, and remnants of a former dam still stand. Neighborhoods encroach on the area, and numerous homes are visible when you drive up to the park, though they'll soon fade from view on the trail.

Along with the obvious draw of the swimming hole in the warmer months, this park has another advantage. Signs about 20 yards from the creek proclaim that from that point on, dogs are not required to be leashed. Fido is free to run and play in the stream just like everyone else, as long as he behaves.

The actual trail begins on the far (east) side of the creek, and crossing should not be a problem. Even in higher water, outcroppings help you stay dry. When the water is rushing, however, err on the side of caution. Even the smallest trickle can become a raging river when the rains come. After crossing the creek, look for the obvious trail to your left. You'll find a clear footpath into the brush and trees. Not far beyond this, you'll reach an intersection. Turn

----

Directions ————————————————→

From the northern part of Austin head south on Loop 360 and turn left at Lakewood. Parking is located off of Loop 360. From the south, reverse the turn direction.

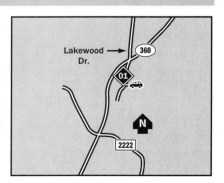

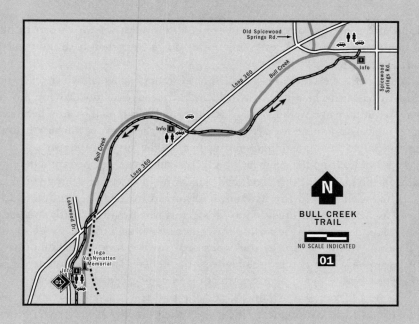

left here, and begin following the creek. Numerous spur trails to your left lead down to the creek; many are no more distinct than a game trail.

After you've hiked 0.5 miles, the foliage to the left opens up to reveal a wonderful view of the creek, about 15 feet below. From this vantage point on the stone escarpment, you can watch the creek's inhabitants, including turtles, fish, and salamanders, depending on where the sun is. The glare will make it a little more difficult to see through the water. Polarized sunglasses may be in order. As you continue hiking toward Loop 360, the creek and trail almost merge as you get ready to pass under the highway. The trail gets extremely narrow as it passes through some very tall grass. Once on the other side, you'll see a brown stake and sign marking the trail. You'll encounter a few more of these markers along the hike.

Once beyond the underpass, the trail widens a little, and the hike is easy from here. Keep an eye on the trees as well as the creek. The abundance of water and cover provide ideal habitat for birds of all types, and cardinals appear to be especially common. The birds dart back and forth across the trail along the entire hike. You'll reach a stone staircase after a mile that leads up to a wrought-iron fence. There is no gate apparent. You'll reach a fork just past this point. Stay to the right.

Roughly 0.2 miles from the fork, you'll cross Spicewood Springs Road and see another park on your left about 30 yards away. Keep going across the road, and cross under Loop 360 again. This is the second creek crossing you'll encounter. Before you cross over the creek and under the overpass, take a moment to look up at the bottom of the road. Several cliff swallows have chosen to build their homes here. The mud nests hang upside down from their base and make for an interesting sight.

You'll cross the creek on several square stones, many of which have been marked by passersby. Here the creek widens as it heads back under Loop 360 and offers a beautiful view. Wading birds like egrets and herons can be seen here in the warmer months and make for a striking contrast to the bustle of the busy highway. From this point, the trail continues north, away to the left of the creek.

At 1.5 miles from the trailhead you'll cross another creek bed for a perennial stream. In the middle of this creek bed stands the most curious thing you'll find on this hike—an old red fire hydrant, undisturbed by anything, and not of any obvious use. Beyond the creek the trail will fork again and is clearly marked by another sign, designating the fork to the right as the hiking trail. Go with the sign and continue to the right. The trail opens up past the fork, and the houses are visible again on your right and the highway on the left. There is also a fence here on the right, with a sign designating the other side as a restoration area.

The trail forks again at 2 miles, and the trail to the left leads to the Spicewood Springs Road parking lot. This is the turnaround spot, unless you brought two cars and left one here.

COMMONS FORD RANCH LOOP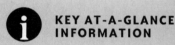

IN BRIEF

Commons Ford Ranch is a preserve in the fast-growing area between the communities of West Lake Hills and Bee Cave. The 215-acre former working ranch on the banks of Lake Austin was acquired in 1983 and now offers respite for walking and enjoying a creekside and open floodplain trail. The upper part of the creek canyon offers exploration of a couple of waterfalls. Don't miss the restored log cabin near the trailhead.

DESCRIPTION

This is an easy ramble through former ranchland along the shores of Lake Austin. The path to the waterfalls along the unnamed creek isn't maintained or marked and is somewhat rougher. The mowed path is easy on your feet and makes for a pleasant stroll. Before you come, be aware that the park is only open Tuesday through Sunday from 1 p.m. to 6 p.m.

Leave the parking area, where live oaks shade the cedar-fenced parking area. Begin walking down along an unnamed stream and pass a sign indicating a picnic area ahead. The

KEY AT-A-GLANCE INFORMATION

LENGTH: 1.2 miles
CONFIGURATION: Loop
DIFFICULTY: Easy
SCENERY: Partly wooded creek bed, open plain, Lake Austin
EXPOSURE: Mostly sunny
TRAFFIC: Moderate
TRAIL SURFACE: Grass, some pavement
HIKING TIME: 1 hour
ACCESS: Free
MAPS: www.ci.austin.tx.us/parks/parkmaps/images/commons_ford_ranch.jpg
FACILITIES: Picnic area

Directions ⟶

From MoPac, Loop Road 1, just south of Lake Austin, take Texas Ranch Road 2244, Rolling Wood/West Lake Hills exit, west. Keep west on 2244, Bee Cave Road, for 7 miles to Cuernavaca Drive. Turn right on Cuernavaca Drive and follow it 0.4 miles to Commons Ford Drive. Turn left on Commons Ford Drive and follow it 1.5 miles to the park entrance. Turn left into the park entrance and follow it 0.4 miles to the trailhead, 100 yards beyond the cabin on your right, just past the short bridge over a creek. The parking area is on your left, and the trail starts on your right.

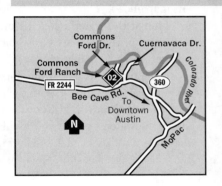

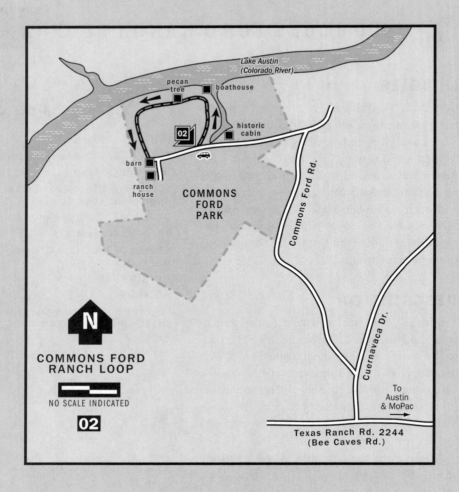

stream is partly shaded by sycamores. Scattered pecan trees shade the surroundings. A wood bridge spans the creek. You'll shortly reach the picnic area, which is complete with a grill. The embayment of the creek is to your right. Lake Austin is straight ahead. The ranch boathouse corners the park. Notice the cypress trees growing at the water's edge. A picnic table lies beneath a cypress tree down here. This part of the lake sees less boat traffic; during colder times of year, the silence and serenity are palpable.

The trail turns left, straddling a pecan-tree-covered hill to the left and the flood plain of the Colorado River to the right. Across Lake Austin, occasional rock outcrops break wooded canyon walls of the dammed Colorado River. These walls rise 250 feet above the water. Look for birds riding the thermals that rise up from the lake and up the canyon wall. Ahead, a single-track path meanders through the grassy floodplain to the lake's edge. The shoreline is protected from erosion by a water wall.

Scenic plains of Commons Ford

The main path turns away from the floodplain and climbs a hill. Ramble through open land toward the ranch barn. Cows may be grazing on the private ranch just across a metal fence from Commons Ford Ranch. Here, turn left onto a paved road. The old ranch house is uphill and can be rented for special events. Follow the paved road, returning to the trailhead.

If you want to explore some more, you may head up the wooded canyon upstream of the trailhead. There are no formal trails, but you are welcome to bushwhack. Just make sure and stay within the confines of the canyon, as the land beyond the canyon rim is private property. However, if you look on your right as you head on the paved road while returning to the trailhead, you will see an unmaintained trail leading toward the canyon through juniper. This path dips into the canyon and flits back and forth across the stream before reaching a wide, low falls. Continue up the creek to reach a taller, narrow falls, more of a true falls by most people's description.

Before you leave, make sure to check out the restored cabin near the trailhead. The notched log work and the chinking hearken back to the early days of central Texas ranching.

03   ROY G. GUERRERO COLORADO RIVER PARK WALK

KEY AT-A-GLANCE INFORMATION

LENGTH: 4.8 miles

CONFIGURATION: Out-and-back

DIFFICULTY: Moderate

SCENERY: Wooded bottomland, lakeside greenway

EXPOSURE: Mostly sunny

TRAFFIC: First half light, second half heavy

TRAIL SURFACE: Pea gravel

HIKING TIME: 2.5 hours

ACCESS: Free

MAPS: None available

FACILITIES: None

IN BRIEF

This greenway trail starts at the east end of Roy G. Guerrero Park, then travels through quiet bottomland along the south shore of the Colorado River past Longhorn Dam to reach Pleasant Valley Road. Pass under the road by tunnel and open to Town Lake, joining the popular route for runners circling Town Lake to end at Lakeside Park.

The trail system at the park is being expanded. Stay tuned as this park grows and you may be able to expand your hike.

DESCRIPTION

Austin is lucky to have many parks as well as dedicated park employees. The namesake of the park where the walk starts is Roy G. Guerrero. Colorado River Park, as it was called, was renamed after Mr. Guerrero, who spent 34 years with the Parks and Recreation Department. He started as an activity leader in east Austin and worked his way up to deputy director. He was very involved in the community and was one of the founders of the Texas Amateur Athletic Federation.

The first portion of Roy G. Guerrero Colorado River Park, now 362 acres, was acquired in 1958. Over the years, other adjacent properties were acquired by donation and

----

Directions

From Interstate 35 in downtown Austin, take Exit 233, Town Lake/Riverside Drive to Riverside Drive, head east on Riverside Drive, and follow it 2.3 miles to Grove Road. Turn left on Grove Road and follow it 1.2 miles to the first circular turnaround near a ball field at the Montopolis Youth Complex portion of Roy G. Guerrero Colorado River Park. The trail starts at the beginning of the turnaround.

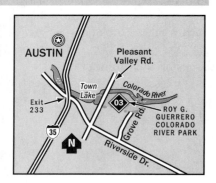

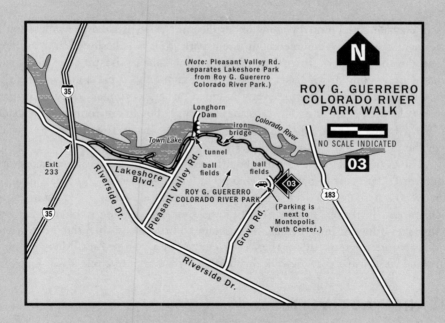

purchase to form the current park. A gravel trail was added, along with ball fields. Now the trail connects with one of the older paths on the south side of Town Lake at Lakeshore Park.

Leave the parking area and ball field to pick up the pea gravel path as it circles around the fields. This area of the park, the Montopolis Youth Complex, opened in 1999. Short bushy trees flank the trail as it passes the park caretaker's home. Dip to a low spot where the trail has been concreted. At 0.5 miles, pass by a clearing through which a petroleum pipeline travels. Stay parallel to the Colorado River, which is just out of sight to your right. Though the sounds of civilization are audible in the distance, the immediate view is of nothing but trees, grass, trail, and sky.

Keep west, passing through this bottomland that was once a dumping ground. Occasional areas of old rusted metal and such can be seen, but the area will continue to improve as more walkers discover this lesser-used path. Ahead, the gravel gives way to concrete as the trail passes over another shallow wash. Veer right beyond this wash. Ball fields are visible on the west side of the park. The trail now leads to an arched iron bridge over a deep, sandy ravine. Circle around the north side of the Krieg Field Softball Complex. Here, the trail comes very near the Colorado River. Walk a few steps toward the water and Longhorn Dam becomes visible, with the Pleasant Valley Road Bridge running over it.

Reach a lighted tunnel passing under Pleasant Valley Road at 1.3 miles. You'll emerge at a seemingly completely different park. This is Lakeshore Park, running along the south side of Town Lake. The grounds and landscaping are very well done. Curve along Town Lake, where willow, cane, and cypress grow along the shoreline. This area of the greenway is much busier, as runners circling around Town Lake pick it up here after crossing Pleasant Valley Road from the north side of Town Lake. To pick up the trails on the north side of Town Lake, just walk over the Pleasant Valley Road Bridge.

The gravel path passes a small boat launch and then curves along Lakeshore Boulevard. Here, a spur path leads to a point with picnic tables. Undulate along a narrow green space between the lake and Lakeshore Boulevard, passing more picnic areas. Just after 2 miles, look for the spur trail leading right to a narrow peninsula jutting far into the lake. Pass around a hostel, and then the green space widens before the trail ends at the western edge of Lakeshore Park. Many runners continue west, using the sidewalk through the urban area to circle Town Lake.

NEARBY ACTIVITIES

Roy G. Guerrero Park has ball fields aplenty. Lakeshore Park has picnic facilities and a boat launch. For more information, call (512) 477-1566 or visit **www .austinparks.org.**

HOMESTEAD TRAIL 04

IN BRIEF

This rugged hike passes through land once owned by Thomas F. McKinney, a frontiersman and entrepreneur who greatly influenced the early history of Texas. Share the path with mountain bikers as it meanders through wooded settings and ends by the remains of the McKinney homestead.

DESCRIPTION

The 744 acres of McKinney Falls State Park was part of a much larger (40,000-acre) tract of land once owned by Thomas F. McKinney, a former Kentuckian who made his living as a trader of cotton and livestock. McKinney, along with Stephen F. Austin and others, helped gain statehood for Texas.

The position of the Texas Parks and Wildlife Department is that McKinney was one of Austin's original colonists, but many other reliable sources suggest that he stopped here in the 1820s only to receive his land grant before moving on to the Galveston area, where he set up a trading business and even worked as a privateer during the Texas Revolution, which he also helped finance to the sum of $99,000. When he did settle in this area between 1850 and 1852 to breed racehorses, he also built one of the first flour mills in the area, powered by the Onion Creek. The ruins of the mill and his house are located on this hike.

KEY AT-A-GLANCE INFORMATION

LENGTH: 3 miles

CONFIGURATION: Loop

DIFFICULTY: Moderate

SCENERY: Old ruins and thick hardwoods

EXPOSURE: Mostly shady with a few openings

TRAFFIC: Light, but watch for mountain bikers

TRAIL SURFACE: Dirt

HIKING TIME: 1.5 hours

ACCESS: $4

MAPS: Available at park office or online at www.tpwd.state.tx.us/ spdest/findadest/parks/mckinney_ falls

FACILITIES: Restrooms, showers, picnic tables, and camping. Many stores are located nearby.

SPECIAL COMMENTS: There are a few open fields filled with wildflowers along the trail. This is prime real estate for rattlesnakes, so stay on the path. Insect repellent is a must on this hike due to the thick ground cover and numerous small insects.

Directions ➡

The park is located 13 miles southeast of the State Capitol in Austin off US 183. Take McKinney Falls Parkway, off US 183 South, which will lead right into the park.

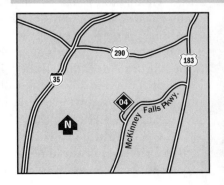

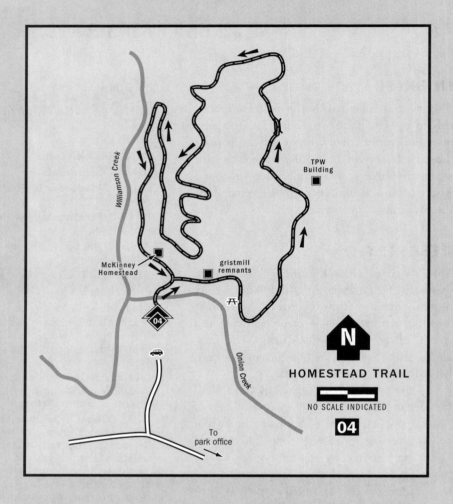

Getting to this hike's trailhead is a little tricky. After you've parked your car and made your way to the creek, you'll encounter the toughest part of this trek—crossing the creek to get to the trailhead. The best way to do this without getting your boots wet is to cross along the waterfall. Depending on the time of year and the recent rainfall, this can be a little tricky. The limestone bed of the creek has several rocks that stick up out of the water, and these can function as stepping stones. This is a good hike to bring a walking staff on, if for no other reason than to balance yourself while crossing the water.

Once you've completed the crossing, an obvious sign marks the beginning of the trail. The Homestead ruins are to the left, and the gristmill's remnants are to the right. Follow the trail toward the gristmill. Mountain bikers tend to start riding the Homestead Trail; hiking the other way (counterclockwise) will give you a chance to see each other and avoid a collision later on down the trail.

The remains of the old gristmill are located less than 200 yards from the trailhead and are marked with an information sign. The stones that made up the mill's foundation are all that remain now, but it once was the first working flour mill in the area. Notice how the creek's path has diverted from the mill since it was originally built.

Just over 0.5 miles into the hike, a concrete picnic table sits to the side of the trail. Not marked on the trail map, this would be a good place to get away from the crowds on an otherwise busy day.

Shortly after the picnic table, the trail narrows to allow for only a single hiker at a time. There are many small, seasonal creek beds that cross the trail, and many are just as wide as the trail itself. As a general rule, keep going straight at these crossings.

The trail forks 0.8 miles from the beginning. Stay to the left; the right fork dead-ends at an open field. You can hear vehicular traffic from across the field, which will remind you just how close you are to the city.

Once you've passed the field, the trees get thick and the birds become very vocal. This part of the trail is great for locating a couple of hard-to-find species. Painted buntings are abundant in these woods, and the occasional indigo bunting will make the walk extremely popular with birders. Their calls will drown out any traffic along the nearby roads. Keep an eye on the trail ahead to see them crossing.

As the trail begins to cut west, a large opening appears on the right, revealing a large building across an open field of wildflowers, about 0.5 miles from the picnic table. This is part of the Texas Parks and Wildlife (TPW) headquarters building. From this point the trail cuts west and back into the thick woods.

A little farther up the trail, you'll encounter another part of the TPW complex. This building is a fitness center for TPW employees. Stay on the trail, and pass the facility on the left.

As the trail turns north, you'll reach a small wooden bridge spanning an empty creek bed. This is a good place to take a break and have a look down the creek for deer, birds, or other active wildlife. This bridge is located just before the halfway point, and the trail starts to narrow even more from here.

Along the trail from the bridge you'll begin to see small signs with arrows pointing the way you came. These are for the bikers' benefit, to keep them on the trail and out of the bushes. You don't have to turn around and go back.

There are a few open areas along the trail where the wildflowers are abundant and the grass is tall, but don't be tempted to wander off the trail. A rattlesnake in the field alerted me to his presence, and you don't want to see them any more than they want to see you.

The tree growth along this part of the trail appears older than in the beginning, and this is a great place to see wildlife. Blue jays and cardinals crisscross the trail and you can hear the buntings' songs (a triple-note tune that stands out from anything else in the area) again. You can also keep an eye to the right for approaching bikers, as the trail loops back a couple of times.

At almost 3 miles into the hike, you'll reach the old McKinney homestead. The ruins have been stabilized to prevent further loss of the historical building. A barbed wire fence surrounds it, so you'll have to appreciate it from a distance. The trail here widens to road size. Look for a small trail to the right. This will take you back to the trailhead and the end of the hike. Once you cross the creek, you might want to stop and soak your feet in it for a while.

HORNSBY BEND LOOP 05

IN BRIEF

This unusual trail circles a wastewater treatment facility with numerous ponds near the banks of the Colorado River. Before you cry foul, realize that this area is a haven for wildlife of all kinds, especially waterfowl and other types of birds.

DESCRIPTION

Talk about turning lemons into lemonade! The Hornsby Bend Biosolids Management Facility provides the unpleasant but necessary job of processing sewage for the city of Austin. Normally outdoor enthusiasts would avoid such a facility. However, this plant near the banks of the Colorado River is a bird-watcher's paradise with trails for viewing the winged critters. A nice 3-plus-mile loop can be made while exploring the Colorado River and its attendant flood plain, along with four ponds where hundreds of birds may be seen. Bring your binoculars and your bird book along with your hiking stick and boots, and prepare for an eye-opening event. Another note: critters such as bobcats, beavers, coyotes, and deer also call the 700-acre facility home. (I saw deer during my hike.)

KEY AT-A-GLANCE INFORMATION

LENGTH: 3.3 miles
CONFIGURATION: Loop
DIFFICULTY: Easy
SCENERY: River flood plain, man-made ponds, buildings
EXPOSURE: Mostly sunny
TRAFFIC: Light
TRAIL SURFACE: Grass, dirt, pavement
HIKING TIME: 2 hours
ACCESS: Free
MAPS: Online at www.hornsby bend.org
FACILITIES: Water, restrooms at administrative offices

Directions

From the Austin airport, take TX 71 east for 1 mile to FR 973. Turn left on FR 973, toward Manor, crossing the Colorado River, following it 1 mile to the Hornsby Bend Biosolids Processing Center. Turn left and follow the wide road as it narrows to pass through a metal gate. Stay with the road for 0.7 miles to near the end of the pavement by Building #10. The hike starts on the gated grassy dike beyond the end of the pavement. The northwest corner of Pond 1 West will be near the parking area.

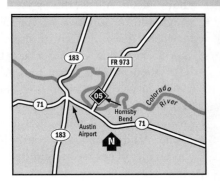

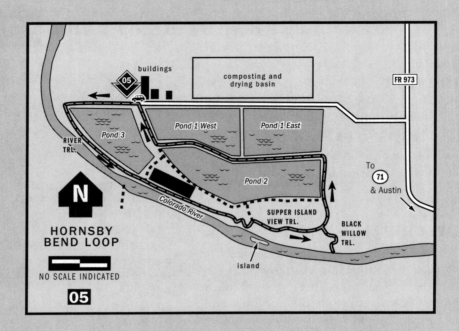

On your first visit, the many buildings, fences, and power lines may make you wonder if you are heading the right way or trespassing. Rest assured, the public is welcome. Leave your parking spot near the end of Pond 1 West, then keep west across the gated dike with an adjacent power line. This is the River Trail. Pond 3 is to your left and is marshy with grasses and trees—unlike the other ponds, which are mostly open. At 0.3 miles, the Colorado River comes into view. A spur trail leads forward to reach the river's edge. This hike, however, turns left along with the dike to continue skirting Pond 3.

You'll reach a greenhouse at 1 mile. Keep behind the building along a paved road that runs between the building and the river; leave the pavement and dip to bottomland. Ahead, the Upper Island View Trail leads to a view of an island in the Colorado. A primitive viewing blind has been constructed. The river habitat will probably have different birds than those in the treatment ponds. Night herons, cormorants, and kingfishers can be spotted along the Colorado.

Return to the River Trail. Ahead, another spur leads right toward the island. On a curve of the River Trail, the Black Willow Trail also leads to the Colorado. Finally, the River Trail leaves the Colorado and heads toward the ponds, reaching the first one at 2 miles. You are at the southeast corner of Pond 2, the longest pond. A bird blind is to your left and is a worthwhile side trip. Many birds may be visible. (There were hundreds of waterfowl in the ponds on my visit.) Season,

weather, and water-level conditions have everything to do with what you will see. On any given day an experienced birder will observe more than 50 species. The most important tip to really seeing birds is to take your time.

The hike keeps north on the paved road to reach a dike between Pond 2 and Pond 1 East. Turn left onto this dirt road, which offers maximum water observation, with ponds all around. Reach the end of the ponds and some outbuildings. Turn right and return to your point of origin, seeing just how lemonade is made from a lemon here at Austin's biosolids treatment facility.

06 MAYFIELD PRESERVE GARDEN WALK AND AMBLE

KEY AT-A-GLANCE INFORMATION

LENGTH: 1 mile

CONFIGURATION: Multiple interconnected trails

DIFFICULTY: Very easy

SCENERY: Formal gardens, creek gorge, lake

EXPOSURE: Mostly shady

TRAFFIC: Moderate—busy

TRAIL SURFACE: Concrete, dirt, rock

HIKING TIME: 1 hour

ACCESS: Free

MAPS: Signboard map at trailhead

FACILITIES: Picnic area, restroom at trailhead

IN BRIEF

This walk takes place at Mayfield Park Preserve, site of the Mayfield-Gutsch Home and Gardens. After touring the homesite and backyard gardens, amble around on a series of short, interconnected trails through the woods along Bull Creek near the shores of Lake Austin.

DESCRIPTION

To call something a hike implies using a determined trail or set of trails in a specific order, heading from point A to point B. Most hikes will also lead you back from point B to point A. Here at Mayfield Nature Preserve, point A is the parking area, and your starting point is set. The problem is getting to point B and exploring the highlights of this area. Mayfield Nature Preserve has many highlights: the Mayfield-Gutsch House and Gardens, Bull Creek and its canyon scenery, a couple of overhanging rock houses, thick woods, and a vantage point overlooking Lake Austin. The problem is the seemingly innumerable short trails that crisscross this preserve. There is simply no way to systematically walk them to see everything. So, just get out here and get lost!

Really, there is no way to be truly lost for more than a few minutes, because the park is bounded on all sides by houses, 35th Street, and Lake Austin. In fact, it is a good place to just amble around, let your feet take you where they may, even if it is to a dead end or a backtrack.

Directions

From MoPac, Loop Road 1 in Austin, take 35th Street west for 0.6 miles, and prepare to veer left just past Balcones Street, staying on 35th Street for 0.2 miles farther. Turn left into the small stone-gated entrance, on your left.

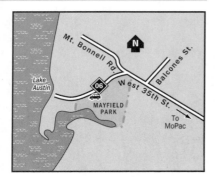

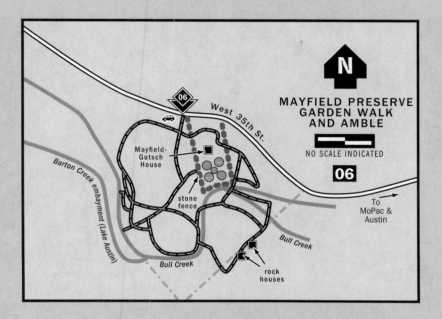

Step back 100 years and learn how Mayfield Park came to be. Alison Mayfield, Texas Secretary of State from 1894 to 1896 and then Railroad Commissioner from 1896 to 1922, purchased the property in 1909. A small cottage was already here, dating from the 1870s. Mayfield used this getaway primarily as a summer cottage. She bequeathed it to her daughter Mary and son-in-law Milton Gutsch in 1922. Milton and Mary began to develop gardens around the house and kept at it for nearly 50 years, building ponds, stone walls, and outbuildings. The house was enlarged as well, ending up as a sprawling cottage. In 1971, the property was bequeathed to the city of Austin for use as a park. In 1994, the park was listed on the National Register of Historic Places. Today you can tour the gardens in addition to walking the mini-maze of trails. The house can be rented out for special functions as well.

The following is a suggestion for exploring Mayfield Nature Preserve. Do not worry about following this route directly, for you will get lost, backtrack, and return to the house and parking area a few times, just as I did. Remember that this is an amble, not a true hike, so just let your feet lead the way.

Leave the parking area and take the visitors' entrance to the house and gardens. An iron gate allows passage beyond the stone wall. Pass by the front of the house, noting the native Texas palms, which lend a tropical look. Head down the

Mayfield-Gutsch House

driveway around to the back of the house. Four concrete ponds lie around a smaller center pond. Benches overlook the ponds. Various small gardens, tended by volunteers, grow between the ponds and the back stone wall. Stroll among the gardens, seeing the varied plant species. Look over the back wall of the backyard. The stone wall is backed against the edge of the canyon wall of Bull Creek, which flows below. You will undoubtedly notice the peacocks roaming about the backyard as well.

After you've finished touring the gardens, look for the stone gate with a bell hanging just beneath a stone arbor near the driveway. Enter the woods beyond the gate. The contrast with the landscaped gardens is startling. Nature grows in organic shapes, sizes, and locations. Cedars and live oaks stand tall over their fallen leaves. The path immediately drops down to a feeder branch of Bull Creek. Walk down the creek and rock-hop over it. Look up at the sheer canyon wall. Do you see the back wall of the Mayfield House gardens? Shortly cross Bull Creek; or you could head upstream on the creek.

The multitude of paths soon becomes evident. All the paths are short, so you can get lost and quickly backtrack—or end up having even more fun. Head left past Bull Creek, and you will come to a trail that leads left to a canyon wall. Cedar steps lead up to a couple of small rock houses. (I imagined someone huddling under the shelter during a thunderstorm.)

Now, start working toward Lake Austin. The dense woods and numerous trails add a confusing aspect to the walk. Remember that Bull Creek leads to the lake. Spur trails end at the water's edge, where you can overlook Lake Austin. One spur leads to a short boardwalk. You can look into the Bull Creek embayment and the houses across the water. A lucky ambler will keep curving around the edge of the preserve and end up at the parking area. Fear not, for 35th Street and the lake will force you back to the parking area. Once at the parking area, consider another look at the gardens and make another amble of this special swath of Austin.

NEARBY ACTIVITIES

The Austin Museum of Art is next door, so you can tour that while you are in the area. The Mayfield-Gutsch House and Gardens can be rented out for special events. For more information, call (512) 327-7723 or visit **www.ci.austin.tx.us/cepreserves/mayfield.htm**.

McKINNEY ROUGHS
BOTTOMS AND BLUFFS HIKE

07

KEY AT-A-GLANCE
INFORMATION

LENGTH: 5.7 miles

CONFIGURATION: Figure-8

DIFFICULTY: Moderate–difficult

SCENERY: River vistas, woods, river bottoms

EXPOSURE: Half sunny, half shady

TRAFFIC: Moderate

TRAIL SURFACE: Pea gravel, rocks, dirt

HIKING TIME: 3 hours

ACCESS: $3/person entrance fee, $1/person under age 14 or over age 65

MAPS: At park office

FACILITIES: Picnic area, restroom at park office

IN BRIEF

This figure-eight loop hike offers views from up high and big trees from down low. Start along the rim of the Colorado River to enjoy some far-reaching vistas. More vantage points can be had on riverside hills. Then dip down to water level, traversing some rich bottomland where massive pecan trees grow. A few last views await on your return to the plateau rim.

DESCRIPTION

McKinney Roughs Nature Park has numerous short trails, and this hike has lots of trail intersections. However, the trail junctions are well marked, so don't get bogged down in trying to figure out where you are. There is a lot to see on this loop, and the many paths take you to some of the best of the Roughs—views of the Colorado River Valley, through rich forests, directly along the Colorado River, and among bottomland where pecan trees grow to staggering sizes. So study the paths, then take off on an enjoyable trek. Note that the hike travels both hiker and hiker/horse trails.

Leave the trailhead by the silo and pick up the Ridge Trail. This all-access path of pea gravel makes a level track along the rim of the Colorado. Short spur trails lead to overlooks complete with contemplation benches. The Woodland Trail soon leaves left—this will be your return route. At just over 0.5 miles, the Valley View Trail leaves right, and ahead is yet another junction. Dead ahead is a vista point

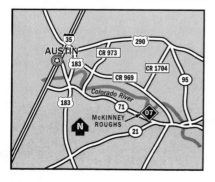

Directions ⟶

From the Austin airport, take TX 71 east for 13.2 miles to reach McKinney Roughs Nature Park, on your left.

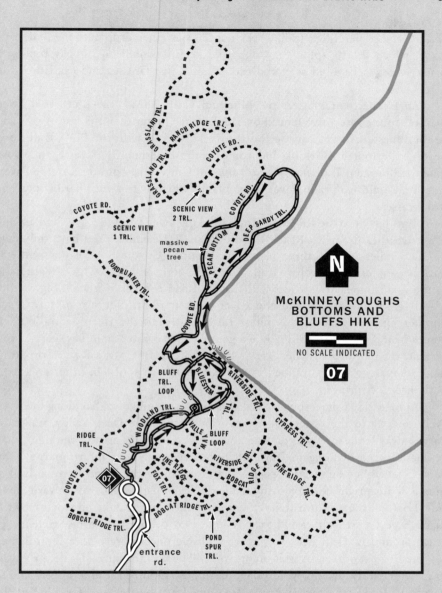

GRASSLAND TRL.

RANCH RIDGE TRL.

COYOTE RD.

COYOTE RD.

SCENIC VIEW
2 TRL.

COYOTE RD.

DEEP SANDY TRL.

COYOTE RD.

SCENIC VIEW
1 TRL.

massive
pecan
tree

PECAN BOTTOM

ROADRUNNER TRL.

COYOTE RD.

N

**McKINNEY ROUGHS
BOTTOMS AND
BLUFFS HIKE**

NO SCALE INDICATED

07

BLUFF
TRL.
LOOP

BLUESTEM
TRL.

RIVERSIDE TRL.

CYPRESS TRL.

WOODLAND TRL.

VALLE
WAY

BLUFF
LOOP

RIDGE
TRL.

RIVERSIDE TRL.

PINE RIDGE
TRL.

COYOTE RD.

07

PINE RIDGE
FOX TRL.

BOBCAT
RIDGE

BOBCAT RIDGE TRL.

BOBCAT RIDGE TRL.

POND
SPUR
TRL.

entrance
rd.

and the end of the Ridge Trail. Check out the view, then drop onto the Bluff Trail Loop, which shortly splits. Stay right and keep downhill on a rocky trail with many switchbacks amid scattered cedars and oaks. Grasses and cacti thrive in places, too.

At 1 mile, you'll bisect the Bluestem Trail. Ahead, the Bluff Trail Loop features four consecutive fenced overlooks, each better than the last. A shortcut to the Bluestem Trail is at the fourth overlook. Stay with the Bluff Trail Loop beyond the fourth overlook and come to the Bluestem Trail yet again. Now, take the Bluestem Trail and drop off the hill you've been on to reach the Riverside Trail amid Colorado River bottomland, which is rife with hardwoods and lush grasses.

Turn left onto the Riverside Trail, working away from the river and around a wet-weather drainage. Reach Coyote Road at 1.5 miles. (You have only covered 1.5 miles after all those path intersections.) Coyote Road is open only to park personnel and is really a trail. Turn right here, and keep with Coyote Road as the Roadrunner Trail leaves left. Coyote Road is open overhead. Big cottonwoods grow along the Colorado River to your right. Not surprisingly, reach another junction at nearly 2 miles. Turn right onto the Deep Sandy Trail. It comes nearer the river, rolling like a gentle roller coaster amid hackberry trees, sycamores, and tangled vines. Pass a little shortcut to Coyote Road. True to its name, the Deep Sandy trailbed is deep and sandy in spots. In other areas, the path bisects clearings.

At mile 2.5, a short spur leads down to a grass and gravel bar along the river. Walk directly to the water—upstream is an island. The Deep Sandy Trail then curves away from the river, passing a gated special events area to the right, then reaches Coyote Road again. Turn left here, beginning your return journey. Traverse a fence line amid large pecans before reaching the Pecan Bottom Trail at mile 3.3. Turn right here, enjoying the level, shady path as it heads toward a hillside. Look for narrow deer trails crisscrossing the bottomland. You won't miss the massive pecan tree—it would take at least two people with arms stretched to reach around it. Drift back toward the hillside once more before returning to Coyote Road at 4 miles. At this point, you will be backtracking a bit before covering new territory. Take Coyote Road, passing Roadrunner Trail and returning to Riverside Trail. Take the Riverside Trail and leave bottomland for good at the Bluestem Trail. Take the Bluestem Trail back to the Bluff Trail Loop. Turn right here and begin covering new terrain, working uphill and passing some stunning views. One grass meadow with a contemplation bench features sweeping views of Wilbargers Bend and beyond.

The Bluff Trail Loop ends to meet the Woodland Trail and the Ridge Trail. Take the Woodland Trail as it dips into thickets of trees and brush. A fantastic vista with a bench is reached just before intersecting the Ridge Trail at 5.5 miles. Turn right here and backtrack a short bit to the trailhead.

NEARBY ACTIVITIES

The Mark Rose Environmental Learning Center offers a variety of educational programs about the outdoors in general and McKinney Roughs in particular. They also have meeting facilities, a large dining room, and dorms. For more information,, call (512) 303-5073, or visit **www.lcra.org/parks/developed_parks/ mckinney_roughs.html.**

08 RICHARD MOYA PARK LOOP

KEY AT-A-GLANCE INFORMATION

LENGTH: 1.5 miles
CONFIGURATION: Loop
DIFFICULTY: Easy
SCENERY: Shaded creek, pecan groves
EXPOSURE: Half shady, half sunny
TRAFFIC: Moderate
TRAIL SURFACE: Pea gravel
HIKING TIME: 1 hour
ACCESS: Free
MAPS: None available
FACILITIES: Restrooms at park

IN BRIEF

Onion Creek, along the southeastern edge of Austin near Austin Bergstrom Airport, is the setting for this loop hike. The mostly level and easy walk travels along the riparian habitat of Onion Creek before circling back to the trailhead through pecan groves. Bring along a lunch: Richard Moya Park has picnic sites galore.

DESCRIPTION

This park was nearly devastated by a flood in late 2001 that was worse than a flood in 1998. Onion Creek went far over its banks. The park office was swept downstream, the ballparks were destroyed, and the park residence took in water almost to the windows. Travis County has had to put considerable time and money into repairing the park. Fortunately for hikers, the gravel walking trail has been repaired and may be expanded in the future.

Onion Creek has endured many such floods over time. Actually, the very shape and life of the stream and the vegetation that surrounds it are specifically adapted for these periodic natural occurrences. The planted

----

Directions

From I-35 in downtown Austin, take Exit 233, Town Lake/Riverside Drive to Riverside Drive, head east on Riverside Drive, and follow it 3.6 miles to Ben White Road/TX 71. Turn left on Ben White Road and follow it 0.3 miles, then veer south on US 183. Follow US 183 south for 2.6 miles to Burleson Road. Turn left on Burleson Road and follow it 1.2 miles to Richard Moya Park, on your right. Start the hike where the entrance road splits in a T.

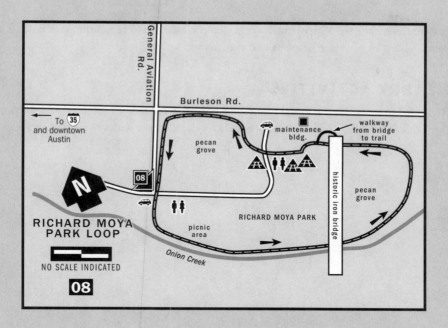

General Aviation Rd.

Burleson Rd.

To 35
and downtown
Austin

08

pecan
grove

maintenance
bldg.

walkway
from bridge
to trail

historic iron bridge

pecan
grove

RICHARD MOYA PARK

RICHARD MOYA
PARK LOOP

picnic
area

NO SCALE INDICATED

Onion Creek

08

pecan groves remained intact following the floods. As noted earlier, however, the park facilities took a major hit during the 2001 flood.

The gravel trail starts at the end of the park entrance road. Walk toward Onion Creek, then begin following the water course downstream. Notice the thick streamside vegetation. If it weren't for these plants, the flooding and subsequent erosion would have been even worse. Trees such as cypress shade the stream and help keep the water cooler in summer and more hospitable for the fauna in and around it. Upstream, the Onion Creek watershed is being surrounded by housing, which normally speeds up runoff and doesn't bode well for this park during the next flood.

The trail circles around a large picnic area shaded by stately hardwoods. This 100-acre park can get busy, judging by all the picnic tables here. Ahead, you can see the large iron-trestle bridge spanning the park floodplain and Onion Creek. This century-old bridge used to span the Colorado River in downtown Austin. Now it is closed to auto traffic. Keep under the bridge, entering pecan groves. The trail curves away from Onion Creek and back under the bridge a second time, now heading westward. Here, a walkway has been built for pedestrians to access the now-closed bridge. Walk the bridge and enjoy the view into Onion Creek. This area is known as Moore's Crossing.

The trail passes next to some picnic shelters and a parking area. Stay on high ground as a large pecan grove occupies the floodplain below. As you walk by, it is easy to detect the trees growing in rows. Keep westward to reach the park entrance road. The trail now turns south and returns to the trailhead.

NEARBY ACTIVITIES

Richard Moya Park has ball fields and courts and picnic facilities. For more information, call (512) 854-7275, or visit **www.co.travis.tx.us/tnr/parks/richard_moya.asp.**

DICK NICHOLS PARK-WESTERN OAKS HIKE AND BIKE TRAIL

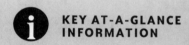

IN BRIEF

This urban hike is set in a relatively new development area. It offers amenities for fitness advocates as well as casual hikers, ranging from fitness stations to picnic tables.

DESCRIPTION

Ideal for families and hikers of all skill levels, this hike begins in Dick Nichols Park. This is a relatively new park, and if everyone takes care of it as they go, it will be easy to keep in its pristine condition. To reach the trailhead, follow the concrete path leading away from the lot until it joins the loop that surrounds the park. At this point, as well as many others, there is a bench and a garbage can.

Turn left and follow the path as it winds its way from the parking lot. Notice the posts with plastic bags to help people take responsibility for their garbage or pets. You'll encounter a fair amount of traffic on this loop, including power walkers, joggers, dog lovers, and the occasional biker, but it will ease up once you get to the Western Oaks Hike and Bike Trail.

Although this is a well-maintained loop, plenty of wild areas surround the concrete path, and your chances of glimpsing some of the area's smaller wildlife in the area are good during the early morning and late afternoon. Squirrels, raccoons, and opossums should be abundant during the twilight hours.

As the vegetation begins to surround you, you might catch a glimpse of a seemingly

KEY AT-A-GLANCE INFORMATION

LENGTH: 2 Miles

CONFIGURATION: Balloon

DIFFICULTY: Very easy

SCENERY: Park playscape, Hill Country vegetation, and a curious cave

EXPOSURE: Mostly shady

TRAFFIC: Moderate

TRAIL SURFACE: Concrete and packed gravel

HIKING TIME: 1.5 hours

ACCESS: The park is open from 5 a.m. to 10 p.m. There are no access fees.

MAPS: None

FACILITIES: Restrooms, public swimming pool, water fountains

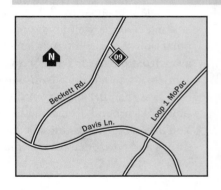

Directions ————————————————➤

Take the Davis Lane exit off of MoPac, and head west. At Beckett Road, turn right and travel north. The parking area is on your right.

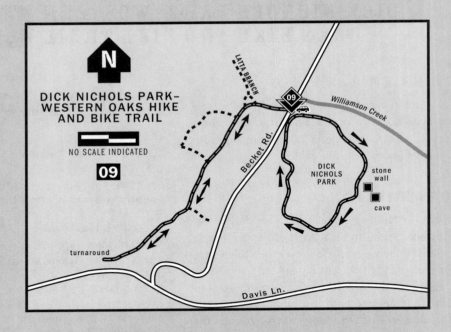

out-of-place stone wall through the trees to your right. You'll be able to see it better about 0.5 miles into the hike. This circular wall encloses the entrance to a cave and serves to keep people out. Though the wall could be easily crossed, you'd be wise to avoid closer inspection of it.

Continuing on, you'll spy some larger oak trees along the second half of the loop that host some of the local bird life, which you'll see as you hike back toward the parking lot. As you hike alongside Beckett Road, you'll see a trailhead sign across the street. This is the start of the second half of the hike. Be sure to look both ways, and cross the street to reach it.

The short boardwalk leads to a trailhead board, which includes a map of the existing trail, as well as the planned trails to come. There are two other entry points on the current trail and a couple more planned. Follow the gravel trail away from the road. You'll see a fork about 0.2 miles from the map board. This is actually a side loop that soon rejoins the main trail.

Less than 0.1 mile from the point where the spur rejoins the main path, the trail forks around a picnic area, and then it forks again around a stand of trees. You'll find numerous fitness stations along this trail, including platforms for doing sit-ups and horizontal bars for pull-ups. Joggers tend to take advantage of this trail for their morning runs, and the sound of footfalls will signal when they are coming your way.

Past the second picnic table area, you'll notice a fork to the left that leads to a small park consisting of another trail sign and a small playscape. Keep to the right and stay on the main trail. You'll be walking behind a row of houses at this point until you see a large concrete ledge on your left, which is actually a drainage ditch. Stay to the right and continue hiking toward the final entry point. You'll cross a dry creek bed before reaching the final entry point along Davis Lane. Another trail sign here marks the end of this hike. Turn around if you don't have someone picking you up, and make your way back to Dick Nichols Park. If you have the time, the swimming pool might be open and worth checking out on a hot day.

10   ONION CREEK LOOP

KEY AT-A-GLANCE INFORMATION

LENGTH: 2.6 miles
CONFIGURATION: Loop
DIFFICULTY: Easy
SCENERY: Onion Creek, wildlife, wildflowers, and birds
EXPOSURE: Shady
TRAFFIC: Moderate
TRAIL SURFACE: Asphalt
HIKING TIME: Less than 1 hour
ACCESS: Open for day use and overnight camping year-round
MAPS: Available at park office
FACILITIES: Restrooms, showers, campsites, and park store

IN BRIEF

Bikers, joggers, and hikers share this long loop around McKinney Falls State Park as it winds through the shady banks of Onion Creek and past more ruins from Thomas McKinney's home.

DESCRIPTION

Explore enough of Austin's nearby trails and you will undoubtedly come across the name of Thomas F. McKinney. Like the Homestead Trail, the Onion Creek Trail lies within McKinney Falls State Park, just inside the city limits.

In addition to establishing the area's first mill, McKinney also bred and raced horses on this land. The improvements here even included a private track, which wasn't the first one he ever built. While in Galveston, where he served in the state legislature, he also built a race course. After moving to the Austin area, he built another one here, across the river from the capital city.

Originally a league of land (about 5,700 acres), the remaining 744-acre state park contains numerous signs of the residence that once stood here. Although the gristmill and homestead ruins are found on the Homestead Trail, the remains of his horse trainers' cabin and long lines of stone fence remain on this path, and they even mark part of the park's boundary.

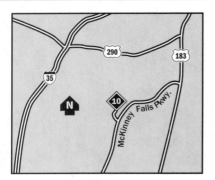

- -

Directions ————————————→

The park is located 13 miles southeast of the State Capitol in Austin off US 183. Take McKinney Falls Parkway, off US 183 South, which will lead right into the park.

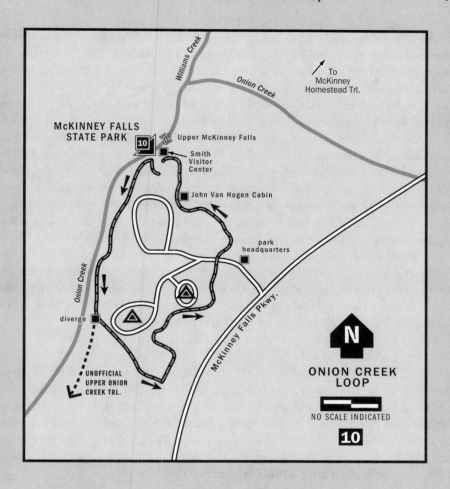

The hike begins at the Smith Visitor Center, where hikers can purchase bird checklists, walking sticks, and other various items from the park staff. At a natural pool where the Big McKinney Falls area of Onion Creek is visible in front of the visitor center, swimmers create the only noise here. The trailhead is located on the south side of the building and is marked with a sign.

Watch for bicyclists as you walk down the path to the right, into the shady picnic area. The path is about 50 yards from the creek, and you'll see several picnic tables spread out under the tall trees. The first 0.4 miles snakes through the picnic and primitive camping areas of the park. At 0.5 miles, the woods get thick, and you get a little closer to the creek. Keep an eye out for the painted bunting, a small, colorful songbird that nests in the park through the summer. They are more abundant on the Homestead Trail but can still be seen here as well.

The trail passes by a stone embankment on the left that serves to prevent further erosion of the hillside. A small foot trail also leads down to the creek on the right. However, continue on the main path, which makes a steep climb as it turns to the left, away from the creek. A sign advises that bikers coming the other way walk their bikes at this point, but keep your eyes open anyway. At the top of the rise a park bench offers a place to sit and rest or watch the birds.

About 1.2 miles into the hike, you'll see another bench off the trail as well as a stone wall that used to serve as the land's boundary. McKinney built the wall in the mid-1800s. A modern fence parallels the wall. The trail forks at 1.7 miles. Turn left and you will end up in the RV campsite area, so take the trail to the right. Not far from the fork you'll see an observation blind made of a wooden bench and wall. Across the trail in a clearing is a bird feeder. Avid birders can use this area, and the wall will allow them to set a spotting scope for close observation.

In the spring, large sections of the tall grass are pressed down by deer birthing their fawns. Attentive hikers can spy the fawns hiding under the bushes or hear them calling to their mothers. These babies are not lost and should be left alone. This is a common mistake made by people trying to help that actually wind up hurting the deer. Please take only pictures of the fawns.

More of the rock fence appears 2.2 miles along the path and still serves as the park boundary. Another bench located near here lets you sit and watch the passersby as well as the deer and birds. The park headquarters is visible through the trees to the right, as are the campsites to the left. The trail crosses the park road at 2.4 miles. Directly across the road are the ruins of the cabin that belonged to John Van Hogen, Thomas McKinney's horse trainer. Cross the road carefully to get a better look. You'll exit the woods after walking 2.6 miles and find yourself back at the Smith Visitor Center. The water fountain inside offers a cool drink, or you could immerse yourself in the creek.

PACE BEND TRAIL

IN BRIEF

Although Pace Bend lacks interpretive information, its unattended and understated nature offers a great deal of appeal to hikers seeking peace and quiet. This place is definitely a well-kept secret for hiking.

DESCRIPTION

Located 30 miles west of Austin, the 1,368-acre Pace Bend Park is one of the more popular water recreation parks in the area. However, if you avoid the shorelines, regardless of the crowds, the solitude just might surprise you. The trails at Pace Bend are primarily little-used maintenance/Jeep roads, providing a wide and easy-to-follow path for most of the hike. There are numerous side trails, created by wildlife or hikers who strayed from the established path, but the main trail is easy to discern from these.

The majority of the hike takes place between stands of trees. Plenty of open space overhead warrants a hat and sunscreen to prevent an otherwise great day from turning into a sunburned nightmare. It doesn't take long for the sun to work its magic, so take all necessary precautions. One other feature of the hike merits a mention: spiders. The arachnids around here are of the extra-large variety and are often found on large webs spanning the trails, so keep an eye out for them both in the air ahead and on the ground below (tarantulas are also prevalent).

KEY AT-A-GLANCE INFORMATION

LENGTH: 6 miles

CONFIGURATION: Out-and-back

DIFFICULTY: Moderate

SCENERY: Lake, woods, and grasslands

EXPOSURE: Moderate

TRAFFIC: Light

TRAIL SURFACE: Dirt

HIKING TIME: 3 hours

ACCESS: Open sunrise until 9 p.m.; $8/vehicle fee

MAPS: None

FACILITIES: None

Directions

From the intersection of RR 620 and TX 71, take TX 71 west 11 miles to RR 2322. Turn right on RR 2322 and travel 4.6 miles to the park entrance.

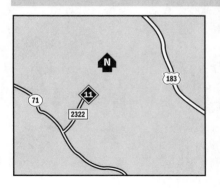

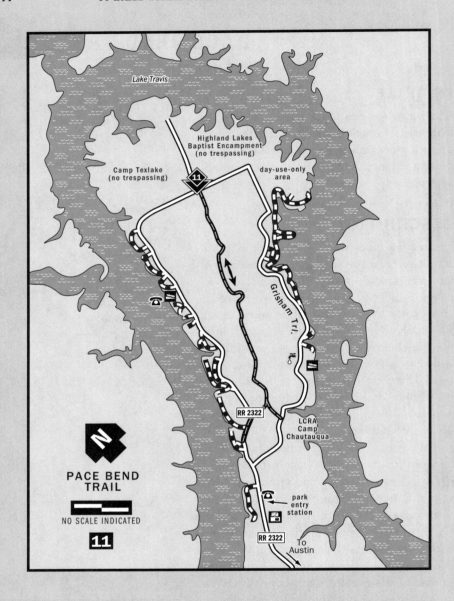

Lake Travis

Highland Lakes
Baptist Encampment
(no trespassing)

Camp Texlake
(no trespassing)

day-use-only
area

Grisham Trl.

RR 2322

LCRA
Camp
Chautauqua

PACE BEND
TRAIL

NO SCALE INDICATED

11

park
entry
station

RR 2322

To
Austin

As you hike along the trail, keep your eyes on the tree lines when not watching for spiders, and you should see plenty of wildlife. The proximity of the trail to Lake Travis is a natural draw for mammals and waterfowl alike. Bring your birding binoculars, and you'll be treated from everything from titmice to pelicans, depending on the time of year. Songbirds and shorebirds populate this area.

The hike starts at the northernmost part of the park. Head south, and about a half mile from the trailhead, you'll reach the first fork in the path. At this point, take the right fork. The hardest part of this hike is to know which forks to take to get the most out of what it has to offer. With that in mind, at the next fork, take the left, and at the third fork take the right. Just beyond this third fork is a T-intersection. The road to the left heads toward the lake and dead-ends into the main park road, so take the path to the right.

About 2 miles from the intersection, you'll come to a fenced-in area, with a water tank and building on the inside. They appear to be in good shape and don't seem to have been abandoned. No other paths lead to it, however, so it remains a bit of a mystery. If you follow the fence around to the left, you'll find the trail. It leads southeast through a small creek valley and ends at a second trailhead on the main road that loops around the park. When you reach this point, turn back and return to the fenced area. When back at the fenced area, head left, and you should see another spur trail heading to the southwest. Take this path, which is a little rougher and overgrown than the rest of the trail. If you want to shorten the hike and you have two cars, a shuttle can be set at the end of this spur trail, which intersects the main loop road. Otherwise, return again to the fenced area.

At the fenced area, head left, where the foliage is sparser, offering good views of the water and the houses on the opposite bank. You will also notice several small trails leading to the left that you might want to investigate in the future, but for now, take your time and continue around the fenced area until you intersect the main trail. Turn left (north) and take your time looking for anything you might have missed on the way down.

12   PINE RIDGE LOOP

KEY AT-A-GLANCE INFORMATION

LENGTH: 4.1 miles

CONFIGURATION: Loop

DIFFICULTY: Moderate

SCENERY: River bluffs, pine–oak woodlands

EXPOSURE: Half shady, half sunny

TRAFFIC: Moderate

TRAIL SURFACE: Dirt, leaves, pine needles

HIKING TIME: 2.25 hours

ACCESS: $3/person access fee, $1 for those younger than age 14 or older than age 65

MAPS: At park office

FACILITIES: Picnic area, restroom at park office

IN BRIEF

This hike explores the McKinney Roughs from high to low and back again. Start along a high plateau to circle around and down to the Colorado River, gaining far-reaching views from the plateau rim. Cruise beside the wide-water course to return via a trail that offers more views. Old home sites and ranch relics can be seen on the way.

DESCRIPTION

In 1995, the Lower Colorado River Authority (LCRA) acquired the land now known as McKinney Roughs and built a first-rate environmental education facility to complement a 1,100-acre preserve along the Colorado River between Austin and Bastrop. Today, the park has 18 miles of hiking and equestrian trails that explore the rugged terrain, which earned the name roughs from the vertical variation that made large-scale agriculture difficult. The steep ravines and thick woods also provided refuge for frontier outlaws.

The park trailhead is a short walk toward the metal silo beside the park office. Find the marked Riverside Trail, and follow a partly wooded plateau environment dominated by cedar trees. At 0.2 miles you'll reach a trail intersection. Keep forward, now on the Pine Ridge Trail. (The Fox Tail Trail leaves to the right, and the Riverside Trail continues left. The Riverside Trail to your left will be your return route.)

Directions

From the Austin airport, take TX 71 east for 13.2 miles to reach McKinney Roughs Nature Park, on the left.

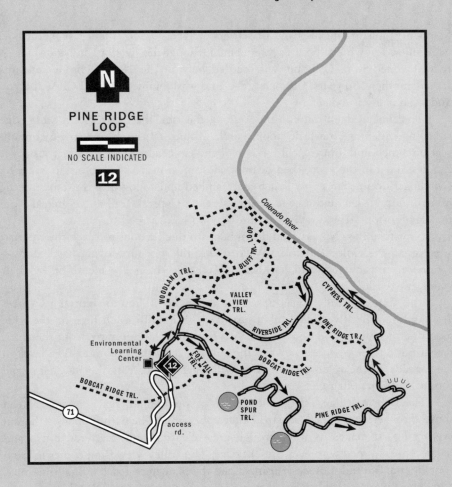

The Pine Ridge Trail cruises along the rim of the Colorado River valley, passing the Bobcat Ridge Trail at just over 0.5 miles. Scattered woodlands break up clearings where cacti sporadically reach above the grass. Ahead, the Pond Spur Trail leaves right to an old stock pond. Large loblolly pines grow in the area. Pass through more clearings, keeping your eyes peeled for remains of an old homestead chimney. A crumbling barn is more evident directly beside the trail.

McKinney Roughs has been home to humans for a long time. Aboriginal Texans were living in the area as long as 8,000 years ago. They ate what the land allowed, cooking acorns and cactus in limestone-slab ovens. Oven remnants helped archaeologists place them here. Later, bows and arrows enabled meat to become more common fare. Grains were also consumed. Their way of life went downhill when European explorers came this way in the 1500s. Then, in the early 1820s,

Stephen F. Austin and his band of settlers arrived. One of them was Thomas F. McKinney, for whom the area was named, though he lived 12 miles distant. A fellow named John Calhoun Wise settled here in the 1850s. His descendants stayed another 100 years. Ultimately the land was obtained by the LCRA, and you and I can enjoy it today.

The Pine Ridge Trail continues along the rim, then traverses a knife-edge ridgeline widening to a little knob. Circle around the knob to reach a contemplation bench and a far-reaching view of the Colorado River Valley at just over 2 miles. Take in the vista, then begin to descend toward the Colorado River by switchbacks on cedar steps. Reach a streambed and follow it a bit, crossing the branch on a bridge, and ascend to intersect the Cypress Trail at 2.5 miles. Note the clay erosion-created ravines on the way up.

Now take the Cypress Trail down beneath thick woods to reach the riparian zone along the Colorado River. Walk among the moisture-loving hardwoods— sycamore, cottonwood, and hackberry. Hackberry trees are identified by their warty gray bark.

The Cypress Trail travels upstream along the Colorado. Exit the Cypress Trail and join the Riverside Trail at just over 3 miles. Turn left here on the wide path open to hikers and equestrians. As you climb the hill away from the river, turn around to enjoy more views of the lands beyond the Colorado. The land on the far side of the river encompasses Wilbargers Bend. Pass the Bluestem Trail coming in from your right.

The Bobcat Ridge Trail comes in from your left on reaching the plateau above the river. Enjoy the level stroll after your climb. The path is open to the sun overhead as it makes its way through grass clearings and scattered brush and cedar copses topped with ever-present oaks. The Valley View Trail comes in from your right at 3.6 miles. Keep cruising along the plateau to reach a final trail junction. The Riverside Trail turns right here. Retrace your steps 0.2 miles to return to the trailhead.

NEARBY ACTIVITIES

The Mark Rose Environmental Learning Center offers a variety of educational programs about the outdoors in general and McKinney Roughs in particular. They also have meeting facilities, a large dining room, and dorms. For more information, call (512) 303-5073, or visit **www.lcra.org/parks/developed_parks/ mckinney_roughs.html.**

RATTAN CREEK TRAIL

IN BRIEF

This quiet and mostly uneventful little hike begins and ends at a neighborhood park—bring the kids and even the grandparents along on this easy trek.

DESCRIPTION

As often happens in hectic schedules, time can be too scarce to get out and enjoy a long day hike. At 1.5 miles, Rattan Creek is an ideal solution to this dilemma. Short enough for a late evening or early morning stroll, it is ideal when time is short or your fellow hikers' endurance is not on a par with your own. Strollers and wheelchairs can easily be accommodated, so all can enjoy this hike.

The trail begins at a playground located on the banks of the Rattan Creek. Except during heavy rains, this stream is usually a creek bed with a few standing pools of water, so there's no need to bring the fishing rod along on this trek. The trail actually starts at the back side of the recreation area. After parking, make your way around this area (or through it, if you've brought the little ones), to start the hike itself.

The gravel trail pretty much follows the contours of the perennial creek and is very easy to traverse. The majority of the trail itself is exposed and surrounded by residential areas

KEY AT-A-GLANCE INFORMATION

LENGTH: 1.5 miles
CONFIGURATION: Out-and-back
DIFFICULTY: Easy
SCENERY: Playscapes, creek bed, and a really neat old tree house
EXPOSURE: Moderate
TRAFFIC: Moderate
TRAIL SURFACE: Gravel
HIKING TIME: Less than 1 hour
ACCESS: Always open
MAPS: None
FACILITIES: None

Directions

Rattan Creek Park is located at the corner of Tamayo Drive and Dallas Drive in north Austin, south of Parmer Lane. From MoPac, head west on Parmer Lane. Pass McNeil Drive and turn left on Dallas Drive, which should be the second left after McNeil. Head south and then turn right onto Tamayo Drive. The park is on the right. Park along the road.

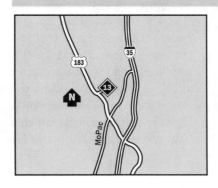

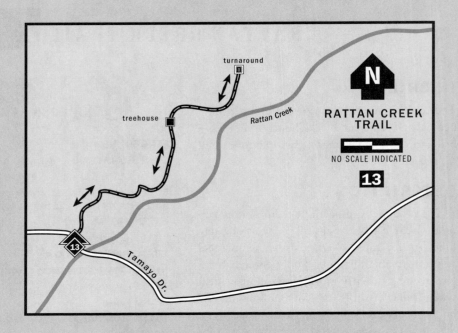

creeping in on the natural environment. Take your time on this trail if you have it, because it could be over before you know it.

Several open fields, though small, should offer wonderful collections of wild-flowers in the spring, which in turn will attract numerous birds and butterflies to the area. As is often the case in new residential areas, some of the wildlife remains, so in the early and late hours, keep your eyes open for opossums, raccoons, and even skunks as they forage for whatever food may be available.

At about the halfway point on the trail, a large oak tree stands on the side of the path. Look into the tree and you'll notice a really neat tree house. The construction seems solid, but use caution if you want to check out the view from it. There's no indication of who built it, but it is on public property, so enjoy it if you want.

The trail continues for about an equal distance to what you've already hiked, ending at Parmer Lane. On the other side of the road new apartments and houses are going in, so the hike pretty much ends here. You could probably explore a little more on the other side, but it won't be as well maintained as what you've already hiked. Perhaps more trail will be added in the future.

After turning around, you've got about 0.75 miles to return to the parking lot. If you're still thinking about climbing up in that tree house, this is your last chance until you come back. If a tree house doesn't bring out the kid in you, nothing will.

SHOAL CREEK HIKE AND BIKE TRAIL   14

IN BRIEF

This trek along a downtown Austin Greenbelt path heads up the watershed of Shoal Creek, passing through several urban parks before ending just beyond an overhanging bluff, 25 city blocks away. The mix of city scenery, stone trail work, and the nature of Shoal Creek mesh to provide a getaway not only for hikers but bikers and runners as well.

DESCRIPTION

An urban greenbelt can only get so woodsy. Austin's city planners did a good job with the Shoal Creek Hike and Bike Trail, creating a pathway that used already-existing parks and connecting them using the narrow strip of land along Shoal Creek. Start this trek at Duncan Park off 9th Street, and then head up to 31st Street, nearing House Park and passing through Pease Park and Dog Park. Short portions of the trail exist on both ends beyond this stretch, but each end currently has problems. The trail between Duncan Park and Town Lake is not connected yet, and the part north of 31st Street travels along a street for a distance before petering out altogether. Both ends may be extended and completed in the future, but for now the following section is the best the trail offers.

🏃 Directions ➡

From I-35, take Exit 234B, 8th–3rd Streets, then take the frontage road to Sixth Street. Head west on Sixth Street for 1 mile to West Avenue. Turn right on West Avenue and follow it 3 blocks to Ninth Street. Turn left on Ninth Street. Duncan Park is on your right. Park on the street by the park. Take the Shoal Creek Hike and Bike Trail north, heading upstream along the creek from Duncan Park.

ℹ KEY AT-A-GLANCE INFORMATION

LENGTH: 5 miles
CONFIGURATION: Out-and-back
DIFFICULTY: Moderate
SCENERY: Wooded city parks, urban creek, scattered forest
EXPOSURE: Partly sunny, partly shady
TRAFFIC: Moderate to heavy
TRAIL SURFACE: Rock, pea gravel, dirt
HIKING TIME: 2.75 hours
ACCESS: Free
MAPS: www.ci.austin.tx.us/parks/traildirectory.htm
FACILITIES: Water fountain, restroom at Pease Park

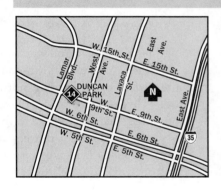

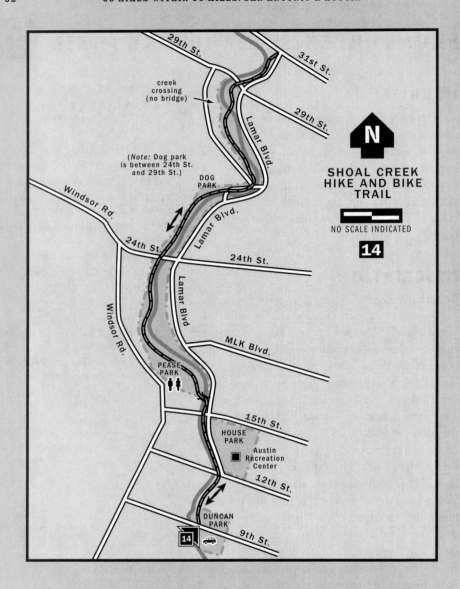

City dwellers will be seen running, biking, or walking dogs along this trail. It is also used as a handy north–south connector for downtown pedestrians. From Ninth Street, begin heading north on the pebbled concrete path east of Shoal Creek. A live oak tree shades the trail entrance. A sign gives the address, 900 West Ninth Street. Across the road to the south is a bike track. Duncan Park is a rolling, grassy expanse dotted with trees and benches. Pass under the Tenth Street Bridge, the first of many bridge underpasses, and keep along a green corridor bordered with stonework to stabilize the trail.

Ahead, across Shoal Creek Boulevard, are House Park and the Austin Recreation Center. Willow, live oak, and brush line Shoal Creek. At just over 0.5 miles, span Shoal Creek on an iron trestle bridge to enter Pease Park. The trail is pea gravel now and divides into two sections here, each circling around the lower end of Pease Park. A small swimming pool and large playground occupy much of the lower end of the park. A water fountain is beside the pool, and a restroom is on the far side of the play area, on the left-hand trail passing through the park.

The primary path keeps forward through Pease Park to rejoin the left trail just before ascending a cedar-covered hill. Dip from the hill and come alongside Shoal Creek again in a floodplain. By now you have noticed the metal-and-chain holes for a disc golf course in the park. Also look for a streamside live oak tree that leans down-current. During its long life, periodic floods have sculpted the tree to grow that way.

The Shoal Creek Hike and Bike Trail now passes under 24th Street. Enter Dog Park, where pet owners are allowed to let their dogs roam without a leash. Watch your feet here as well as in the surrounding wooded floodplain. The trail shortly crosses Shoal Creek Boulevard, at this point not much more than a quiet park road. A hill to your left and the creek to your right pinch the pathway, until the trail is forced to cross Shoal Creek at just over 2 miles. There is no bridge. Shortly pass under 29th Street, coming to the most scenic part of the path. A craggy, dark bluff rises to the right of the way. Boulders have fallen off the bluff, creating a mosaic of rock dotted with ferns and moss. The trail abuts the bluff, then travels under the overhang on a section that is sheer enough to require handrails. Suddenly turn away from the creek and emerge onto 31st Street, a vastly different scene than what you've just passed through. This is a good turnaround point.

If you want to continue on the trail, turn left and follow 31st Street past houses, then dive left into the creek bed on a pebbled concrete path. The trail continues along Shoal Creek to just beyond 38th Street for the time being; with any luck, it will be finished in the future.

NEARBY ACTIVITIES

Pease Park is the most developed park along the Shoal Creek Hike and Bike Trail, with play areas, picnic tables, and a disc golf course. For more information, call (512) 974-6700 or visit **www.ci.austin.tx.us/parks.**

15 SLAUGHTER CREEK TRAIL

KEY AT-A-GLANCE INFORMATION

LENGTH: 2.4 miles

CONFIGURATION: Loop

DIFFICULTY: Easy

SCENERY: Public park playscapes, Slaughter Creek, birds and wildlife, and a karst

EXPOSURE: Moderate

TRAFFIC: Moderate

TRAIL SURFACE: Gravel, dirt, concrete

HIKING TIME: 1.5 hours

ACCESS: Always open

MAPS: None

FACILITIES: None

IN BRIEF

Although located in a milder park environment, this trail offers some rougher terrain as well as a very interesting geological feature. If you don't know what a karst is, this hike will fill in the gaps for you.

DESCRIPTION

The trails in the 546-acre Slaughter Creek Park are mainly large loops around the soccer fields. Primarily used for jogging and walking by local residents, it is useful for a change of scenery, or even change of pace, from some of the more strenuous trails in the area. Much of the hike takes place on a wide Jeep trail, and this is where the walk starts. In the beginning the trail leads both left and right. Go left down the Jeep trail to begin, and you'll return from the right when you've completed the loop.

The trail continues in an almost straight path for about 0.75 miles, at which point you'll make a turn to the right with the path. When you reach the creek, you'll see another Jeep road crossing it, but the one you're on doesn't appear to continue on the other side. There is another trail here that heads toward the creek, and this is the trail you will take. When you reach the creek, you'll cross it. There is a concrete walkway crossing the creek, so getting over the water is no problem at all. Here and at most points of the hike, you are within sight and earshot of the soccer fields. On game days, the solace of the park will not be as evident as

----

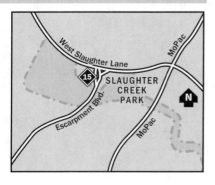

Directions

Head south on MoPac, take the Slaughter Lane exit, and head west. The parking area is on the left side of the road, and the park is on the right.

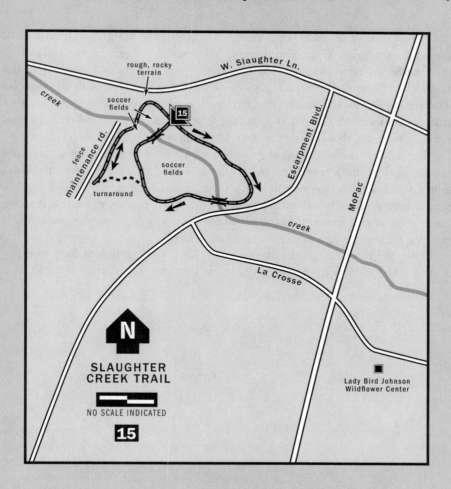

when you can catch it on off-peak hours. Because many teams and leagues use the facilities, there is no real way to know ahead of time when it will be in use.

The trail continues west now for about 0.5 miles along the crushed-gravel perimeter of the soccer complex, then turns north back toward the trailhead. Shortly after this turn, you'll see a chain-link fence near one of the soccer fields and a playscape. If you investigate a little closer, you'll see a hole in the ground on the other side. This, however, is not just a hole—it is a karst.

A karst is a sink, or cave, formed by underground streams that dissolve the rock beneath the surface. The water supply in karsts is very susceptible to contamination. This is one reason for the fence. The other reason is more obvious: to protect people from falling into the hole. Whatever your reason, don't cross the fence.

When you've finished examining this geological feature, continue back toward the trailhead. When you do reach it, turn left, taking the trail you passed up at the beginning of the hike. The Jeep road disappears about 0.2 miles past the trailhead and becomes extremely rocky—be careful so you won't be too rough on your ankles. When you reach the next creek crossing, you won't find another concrete walkway. You'll have to negotiate it by hopping across on the rocks (and there's something about doing this that just brings out the kid in everyone).

From here, the trail hugs the sideline of a soccer field but then continues straight back along a fence and maintenance trail. This area is currently being built up and will change a great deal in the years to come. When you reach a point where you really can go no farther, turn back, play at the creek crossing again, even skip a stone or two, and make your way back to the trailhead. If there's a game on, and you like soccer, stick around.

Though by no means difficult, this hike is ideal for beginners or for a weekday evening when you just have to get outside and don't feel like doing yardwork.

ST. EDWARDS PARK TRAIL   16

IN BRIEF

Often overlooked, this trail is a gem of the Austin area. Chances are, if you've hiked the Bull Creek Trail in this book, you walked right past this one and didn't even know it.

DESCRIPTION

This hike begins in the parking area on Spicewood Springs Road, right next to a huge stand of cacti—more than ten feet in diameter. Many other smaller groups exist along the other side of the trail, betraying the rocky nature of the soil underneath.

From the parking area, head down the trail to a T-intersection, where you'll turn right. The first part of this trail meanders through open fields that host numerous wildflowers in spring and summer. Up ahead, stands of trees replace the open fields.

The majority of this hike takes place in a bend along Bull Creek. As you approach the creek, at the first fork or T-intersection, bear left to continue to the creek. When you reach a four-way intersection, go to the right to parallel the creek, which contains interesting salamanders.

Once you're hiking along the creek, the trail is easy to follow. Waterfalls are located in several spots along the creek; the first offers an interesting sight: a tree standing with a saw blade stuck in it. Either the lumberjack was too uninspired to finish the job or something more important came up.

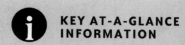

KEY AT-A-GLANCE INFORMATION

LENGTH: 2 miles
CONFIGURATION: Out-and-back
DIFFICULTY: Easy
SCENERY: Creek, trees, and pet owners
EXPOSURE: Mostly shady
TRAFFIC: Light
TRAIL SURFACE: Dirt
HIKING TIME: 1 hour
ACCESS: Always open
MAPS: None
FACILITIES: None

Directions ———————————➤

From TX 360, North Capital of Texas Highway, on the north side of the Colorado River in Austin, take Spicewood Springs west for about 2 miles. The parking area is on the left. It's small, so keep your eyes open.

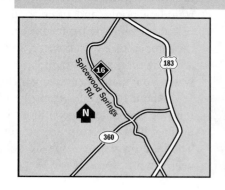

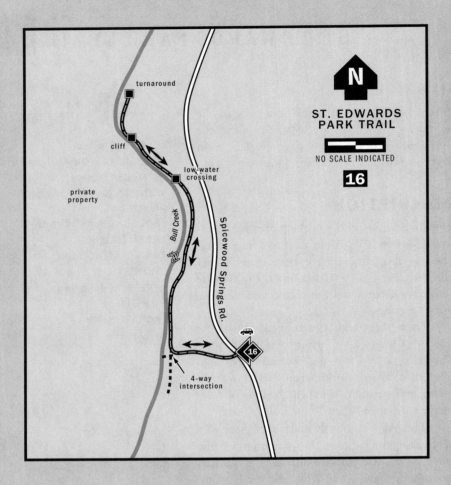

Past the tree with the saw blade in it, you'll encounter an obvious fork in the trail. At this point continue left, along the creek. The next waterfall is really worth the trek. The water here rushes through a slot at a speed much faster than the surrounding pools, and offers both a visible and audible contrast. If you've ever fished for rainbow trout, this area looks like prime territory for them, except for the temperature of the water, so if you're a long-rodder, don't get excited. There are, however, several tadpoles and small frogs in the pool and on the rocks, so watch your step when taking a closer look.

About 0.75 miles from the trailhead, you'll reach a low-water crossing that must be negotiated to continue. This point on the trail is very close to Spicewood Springs Road, so keep an eye out for wayward drivers when crossing the creek. The land on the opposite side of the bank is on private property, so avoid it to keep from trespassing.

Near the 1-mile point, there is a small side spur that leads to an overlook of the creek and an impressive sheer rock wall on the other side. Take a breath, and a picture, before proceeding back to the main trail.

When you reach the point where the trail seems to end, it does. It dead-ends on the road and leaves no sign of continuation on the other side. This is the point where you turn around and head back to the parking area.

17   TOWN LAKE TRAIL

KEY AT-A-GLANCE INFORMATION

LENGTH: 7.2 miles
CONFIGURATION: Loop
DIFFICULTY: Easy
SCENERY: Lake, capitol building, and abundant greenery
EXPOSURE: Open–shady
TRAFFIC: Heavy
TRAIL SURFACE: Paved
HIKING TIME: 3 hours
ACCESS: Open
MAPS: None
FACILITIES: Restrooms

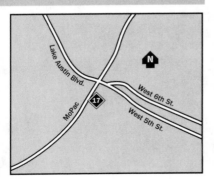

IN BRIEF

This is by far the best-known and, as a direct result, the busiest trail in the Austin area. Hikers, bikers, and meanderers alike share this trail located in the heart of the state's capital. Watch kayakers and boaters play in the water while viewing some of the official buildings of the political center of Texas.

DESCRIPTION

To begin the long loop around the lake, hike east, though there will be opportunities to turn around if the hike proves to be too long. As you walk, you're heading toward the heart of Zilker Park. Along the way you'll be able to see the park's soccer fields to your right, and you'll cross the narrow-gauge railroad tracks used by the popular Zilker Train.

The tree cover increases at this point and stays with you for a while, as you make your way to the confluence of Barton Springs and Town Lake. When you reach this point, you'll find a gazebo and a water fountain if you feel like taking a rest. There is also a good stretch of shoreline for interacting with some of the not-so-wild life. If you have some older bread lying around the house, bring it along to share with the ducks here. They'll appreciate it, and it's good for taking your mind off of other things as well.

Directions

The hike begins under the MoPac bridge, which is obviously located right off of MoPac. Other parking is available, but this is the most convenient. By parking under the MoPac bridge, you're able to avoid what seems to be constant construction going on around the heart of the city.

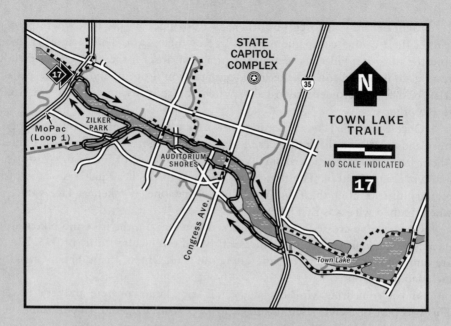

When you're finished at the gazebo, the trail turns south, along Barton Springs, and makes its way to an arched foot bridge that crosses the tributary, then heads back north to the lake. When you reach the lake again, the path turns right and makes its way toward Lamar Boulevard. A new bridge for crossing the road will make it easier for hikers to get across.

The park area at this point is known as Auditorium Shores and is the location of several concerts and events each year. Austinites love their music, and this is only one of many outdoor venues available to enjoy it. Along this section of the trail stands a statue of one of Austin's favorite sons. Stevie Ray Vaughn's guitar style took the music world by storm, and his brilliant career was cut tragically short in a helicopter accident.

You've hiked roughly 2 miles at this point, and it is a good place to turn back if you want to cut things short. If not, keep heading east toward Congress Avenue. Once you've crossed it, the trail runs into an apartment complex, but the hike doesn't have to end. Keep making your way toward Riverside Drive and I-35. The sidewalk here is right next to the road, and the motorists are less aware of you than you are of them. Use caution, because they aren't driving particularly slowly. This is also where you'll encounter the steepest incline in the hike. Persevere through this less-than-peaceful area, because the payoff is worth it.

Right before you reach I-35, there is a dog park on the left, where people can let their canine companions roam free of their leash. This is another good spot for a break if Fido has been tugging on your arm for the past 3 miles. While resting, look ahead toward the interstate and you'll notice the separate pedestrian bridge that crossed Town Lake. When you're ready, this is how you'll get to the other side.

Once across the lake, the setting turns back to a more natural environment of trees and grass, and the traffic here is some of the lightest that you'll encounter. About 0.5 miles from the crossing, you'll reach a couple of interesting historical markers along the trail. The first marks the spot of the headquarters of the fifth military district after the Civil War. The second one, if taken at face value, is where barbed wire was first put into use.

Once you've crossed under Congress Avenue again, the foot and bike traffic increases but remain much more pleasant than the vehicular traffic of I-35. There are numerous side trails to explore along the lake. One of them, Shoal Creek, is included in this book.

As you're nearing MoPac again, you'll see a large concrete and iron tower. This was part of facility used to ferry clay over from the south side of the Colorado River, long before this became a recreational area.

Once you reach MoPac, cross over the lake on the pedestrian bridge and make your way to your car, or take on the Shoal Creek hike before calling it a day, if you've got the energy and the inclination to do so.

TURKEY CREEK TRAIL   18

IN BRIEF

Emma Long Metropolitan Park is the setting for this hike. Travel up the canyon of Turkey Creek, where the path crosses the clear waters of Turkey Creek numerous times. The fern wall of the creek canyon is a highlight before the trail leaves the canyon, traversing the rim on its return journey.

DESCRIPTION

This fun trail explores the lush canyon of Turkey Creek, where cedars, oaks, and sycamores form a nearly continuous tree canopy. Sheer rock bluffs and sloping, wooded walls lead down to crystal clear Turkey Creek. Leave the parking area and immediately enter a grove of cedar trees with their interconnected branches forming a dark canopy. The forest floor is littered with rocks mixed with grass and brush. Drop to cross Turkey Creek near City Park Road. This is the first of numerous creek crossings, which can be easily made in times of normal flow. However, if you can't make the first rock-hop, turn back. Seventeen more such crossings await.

Turn upstream, passing an attractive picnic area. The sky penetrates the canyon in places, lighting the occasional stream pools. The deeper pools have a bluish cast. Take a close look and see how easily you can peer into the clear water. In other places, Turkey

KEY AT-A-GLANCE INFORMATION

LENGTH: 2.5 miles
CONFIGURATION: Balloon
DIFFICULTY: Moderate
SCENERY: Wooded creek canyon
EXPOSURE: Mostly shady
TRAFFIC: Moderate, busy on warm weekends
TRAIL SURFACE: Cedar shavings, rocks, dirt
HIKING TIME: 1.25 hours
ACCESS: $5 access fee, $8 on weekends
MAPS: Available at park fee station 1 mile beyond trailhead, or online at www.ci.austin.tx.us/parks/park maps/images/emma_long.jpg
FACILITIES: Water, restrooms at main park area on Lake Austin, picnic area near trailhead

---

Directions

From MoPac, Loop Road 1, take FM 2222/ Northland Drive west for 4.1 miles to City Park Road. Turn left on City Park Road, and travel 4.8 miles to the trailhead. The trailhead is 0.3 miles past a yellow park gate, then just past the bridge over Turkey Creek, on the right.

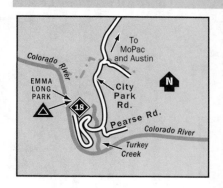

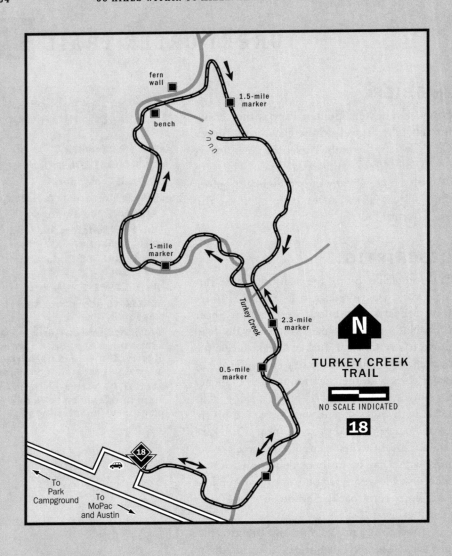

Turkey Creek

Creek glides shallow and swift over wide rock flats. Small cascades offer an inviting visual and audio appeal to the walk. The narrowness of the canyon lends an intimate wilderness feel. The canyon walls alternately lower where dry washes feed into the main creek canyon.

The fords come frequently. On most crossings, natural stepping stones have been laid across the creek. After the fourth crossing, you will reach the half-mile marker—literally a marker that tells you how far you've walked. Cross one more time before reaching the loop portion of the Turkey Creek Trail. Leave left, immediately crossing Turkey Creek, then cross three more times before reaching the 1-mile marker on the inside of a stream curve.

The canyon widens, and the forest opens somewhat. Above, rocks and boulders are sprinkled on the hillsides. In other places, the canyon wall is plainly visible. Three more creek crossings lead you to the fern wall. Here, the moist and cool canyon wall supports a fern colony, resulting in a draping green swath hanging over the creek bed. A contemplation bench enhances the setting, allowing you to absorb the atmosphere of this lush locale. Look for moss growing on the horizontal branches of live oaks as more evidence of this green abundance.

Beyond the fern wall, turn away from Turkey Creek to ascend the side of the canyon. Here, the forest immediately has a more arid look. Scattered cedars grow their limbs down to ground level, side by side with grasses and limestone. Take a closer look at the rock and see how it has eroded into sharp edges in many spots. The sharp rock made me glad that I wasn't wearing sandals. Cacti take their place in the level areas of the canyon rim as well.

Pass the 1.5-mile marker, then reach a side trail leaving to the right. Take this short path to the edge of the canyon. Here, you can look down on the forest below, noting the wooded swale indicating the canyon depth and location. The trail walking is easy now and drifts closer to the canyon rim, ultimately descending a rocky path back down to Turkey Creek. The downhill trail is broken by cut cedar logs that prevent erosion and add steps, making the walk easier.

End the loop portion of the Turkey Creek Trail, backtracking downstream, making the stream crossings again. Pass the 2-mile marker, then the 2.5-mile marker. Make the final of the 18 creek crossings, returning to the trailhead.

NEARBY ACTIVITIES

This city park offers picnicking, camping, fishing, boating, and swimming. For more information, call (512) 974-6700 or visit **www.ci.austin.tx.us/parks/park directory.htm.**

WALLER CREEK TRAIL 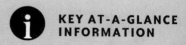 19

IN BRIEF

This urban greenbelt travels through down-town Austin. The stone walkway bridges Waller Creek numerous times on its southbound journey from Waterloo Park near the University of Texas (UT) campus down to Fifth Street. Even though this is an out-and-back hike, multiple parallel paths along Waller Creek can add variety to the walk.

DESCRIPTION

This is not a dirt path through the woods. It is instead an amazing amount of stonework in and around the bed of Waller Creek, which flows through downtown Austin. The city has done a lot to make this trail work, as it snakes below and between many buildings, streets, and businesses. Plans are afoot to turn this trail into a bona fide river walk, à la San Antonio. Take your time, and appreciate the numerous bridges and trail underpasses. Waller Creek is never far away, so, if the rains have been pouring, stay off this flood-prone path.

Pick up the Waller Creek Trail near the corner of 15th Street and Red River Road. The trailhead is at the north end of Waterloo Park near the Ronald McDonald House. This city park has a little green space and picnic tables in addition to the Waller Creek Trail. Stone steps flanked by stone walls descend to

KEY AT-A-GLANCE INFORMATION

LENGTH: 2 miles
CONFIGURATION: Out-and-back
DIFFICULTY: Easy
SCENERY: Creek, stone bridges, urban buildings
EXPOSURE: Mostly open
TRAFFIC: Moderate–heavy
TRAIL SURFACE: Stones, concrete, pea gravel
HIKING TIME: 1.2 hours
ACCESS: Free
MAPS: Online at www.ci.austin.tx .us/parks/parkmaps/images/ waller_creek.jpg
FACILITIES: None

Directions

From I-35, take Exit 235, University of Texas/ MLK and 15th Street. Head east on 15th Street and follow it 0.2 miles toward the university campus to reach Red River Road. Turn left on Red River Road and park on the street next to Waterloo Park. On weekends, you can park in any of the nearby state parking lots for free.

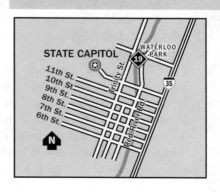

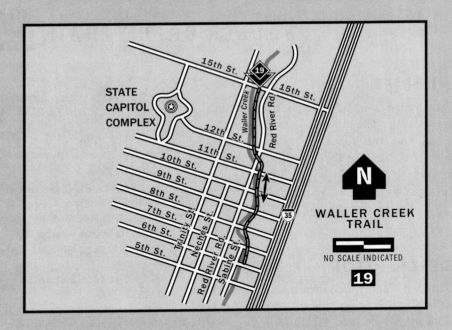

creek level. Head south, downstream, along Waller Creek. (You can also wind through the UT campus upstream along Waller Creek using a variety of campus walkways.) Immediately, you'll begin to appreciate the stonework that lends a picturesque, almost medieval look to the Waller Creek Trail. You will also notice that sometimes parallel paths run on both sides of the trail, especially through Waterloo Park. (Austin was originally known as Waterloo.)

Immediately cross Waller Creek on the first of innumerable bridges. Spur trails connect to the streets above. Pass under 12th Street, the first of many underpasses. Bats are known to live under these bridges.

Buildings and businesses extend directly to the creek's edge. Symphony Square is in one such urban canyon. Here, a portion of the Austin Symphony sometimes plays on a creekside stage. On the far side of the creek, enthusiasts gather on stone outdoor seats to listen.

Waller Creek Trail isn't all about artificial attractions. Look for nature's handiwork, too. Willow trees cling to the edge of the stream. Waller Creek has carved, wide, whitish stone flats in the creek bed. Look closely at the rock patterns that aeons of water and time have worn. Listen for the song of the water as it flows over the rocks in small cascades during times of flow. Unfortunately, the Waller Creek watershed will catch urban trash after a rain, and you will undoubtedly see the results of improperly deposited litter.

Some office buildings have enhanced their landscaping along Waller Creek, adding gardens. Other businesses, especially bars and restaurants, have added patios to overlook the water course. Keep in mind that you can incorporate a meal or beverage into your walk.

I couldn't help but wonder what Austin's founders would think about Waller Creek today. Edwin Waller was sent to this area in 1839 to lay out the city and build temporary government headquarters. Waller later became Austin's first mayor. One of his surveyors supposedly named the creek in Waller's honor. The development of downtown and the University of Texas has made Waller Creek a bona fide urban stream. However, the Waller Creek Trail makes the most of what the city was left to work with in our day and age.

Leave the creek bed to climb by steps to Eighth Street. Cross the avenue, then pick up the trail again as it curves along Waller Creek. A tunnel passes under Sixth Street and steps also lead up to the street. Many bars and clubs are along this street. The final block of the walk passes along the creek, past stone sculptures through which fountains flow. The trail rises to Fifth Street at 1 mile. The trail is disjointed between here and Town Lake to the south, breaking up the continuity and flavor of the walk. In the future, the trail may be completely connected to the trails around Town Lake.

NEARBY ACTIVITIES

Waller Creek courses through downtown Austin, which offers an array of restaurants and entertainment venues.

20   WALNUT CREEK TRAIL

**KEY AT-A-GLANCE
INFORMATION**

LENGTH: 2 miles

CONFIGURATION: Loop

DIFFICULTY: Easy

**SCENERY: Park environment—trees,
birds, and dog owners**

EXPOSURE: Moderate

TRAFFIC: Moderate

**TRAIL SURFACE: Natural stone,
gravel, and dirt**

HIKING TIME: 1 hour

ACCESS: Open 8 a.m.–10 p.m.

MAPS: None

**FACILITIES: Restrooms, athletic
facilities, and swimming pool**

IN BRIEF

Located in far north Austin, this metropolitan park offers not only hiking trails and the usual baseball diamonds and basketball courts, but also the chance to see something not too common in this part of the world: a cricket match.

DESCRIPTION

Purchased by the city in 1964, the park used to be part of a farm owned by the Gracy family. This part of town is close to the environmental region known as the Black Soil Prairie and was probably ideal for crop growth. There are abundant picnic tables if you want to make a day of the outing, and plenty of garbage cans to keep the area litter free.

This park is rife with trails and side paths, with more landscape than you could probably explore in a single outing. There are several creek crossings that, depending on the recent rainfall, can either be crossed without getting damp or may require wading in up to your ankles. Prepare accordingly. These crossings and their approaches can be steep and muddy, so allow enough time to avoid being stuck on the trail after dark.

The trail heads south out of the parking lot, and soon reaches a T-intersection, where the path widens and offers you the option of going left or right, along the ridge above the Tar Branch of Walnut Creek. Go right. Shortly along the path you'll reach the first of many forks in the trail. At this point, take the right and head through the thick trees ahead. Once

----

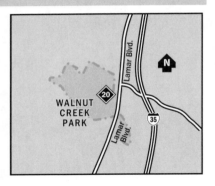

Directions ————————————→

The entrance to the park is located on Lamar Boulevard, between Yager and Braker lanes, west off I-35 North, Exit 244.

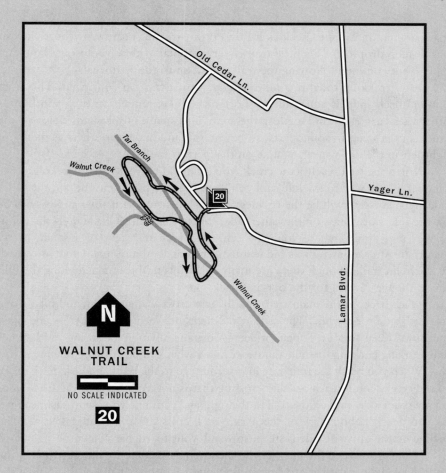

**WALNUT CREEK
TRAIL**

NO SCALE INDICATED

20

through the dense woods, you'll see a chain-link fence and maintenance shed on your right. Just past the shed, the trail cuts to the left and crosses the previously mentioned Tar Branch of Walnut Creek.

On the other side of the creek you'll come to another fork in the trail. Again, continue right. Once again, you'll enter some dense woods, and the trail will climb a bit, emerging from the small stand of trees on top of a hill. From this vantage point, you can see the neighborhood to the northwest of the park, and off to the north stand several open grassy meadows and fields—common sights in the Black Soil Prairie region and a quite a contrast to the more common Hill Country ecosystem.

When you reach the third fork, the trail to the right leads out of the park and into a residential area, so take the fork to the left this time and hike along the main branch of Walnut Creek as it flows downstream. A side spur shortly ahead has a steep drop-off. This little trail is very popular with adventurous mountain bikers, but continue following the trail you're on to the southeast.

After trekking roughly a mile, you see a side trail on your right. This is an out-and-back spur. If you want to shorten the hike, remain on the main loop—otherwise, turn right and explore the spur. This smaller trail winds down to the creek and is steep in some parts, so be careful, and make sure there is plenty of light left in the day when you take on this part of the hike.

When the trail reaches the creek, you'll find a flat, rocky sandbar. Follow the sandbar all the way to the left, and you'll see that the trail continues on the other side. This crossing will be the trickiest of this hike, so take it slow and easy to be on the safe side. Once on the other side, follow the trail as it parallels the tributary system uphill, where you'll be rewarded with the sight of a small, pretty waterfall. After enjoying this hidden gem, turn around and make your way back to the main trail. Though there are many side trails in the area and along the hill, this is the big reward for the out-and-back spur.

Once back on the main trail, you'll again cross Walnut Creek and hike along its north side for a while. The terrain alternates between stands of trees and open meadows. Keep your eyes open for deer—does and fawns in the spring and summer and sparring bucks in the fall. You never know what you'll get to see in an area like this. When you reach the four-way intersection, go to the right and head back down to the creek. You'll reach another crossing that is not as difficult as the first. Once on the other side, stay on the trail to the right and continue your southeast heading. As you near the boundary of the park, you'll cross the creek one last time. The incline on the opposite side is steep, so watch your footing as you go.

When you reach the apex of the incline, you'll come to another fork in the path. The right leads toward Lamar Boulevard and out of the park, so take the left. This section of the trail is larger and flatter than most of the trails and shows signs of more traffic than the other sections. As you follow the trail back to the northwest, you'll again find yourself on the ridge overlooking the Tar Branch. When you reach the trail you entered on, take the right and return to your car, or get out the ice chest and make use of one of the picnic tables—that's why they're here.

WILD BASIN TRAIL

IN BRIEF

Wild Basin offers a wide variety of plant life and terrain within its 227 acres. With views of Bee Creek, portions of the Black-Capped Vireo Preserve, and extensive interpretive information, plan on spending the better part of an afternoon on this hike.

DESCRIPTION

The Wild Basin Wilderness Preserve began as the bicentennial project of seven women who were members of the environmental group Now or Never. They originally attempted (unsuccessfully) to lobby the Texas Parks and Wildlife Department to make the area a state park. They were eventually able to acquire money through fund-raising, private donations, and matching grants to purchase the area and set it aside as a safe haven for local plant and wildlife. The area opened to the public in the early 1980s for use as an outdoor classroom and educational area.

The hike begins at the large map display near the collection box on the North Holler Trail. The beginning of the hike slopes down at a not-too-steep angle. Along this descent there is a creek valley to your left, as well as another ridge to the north of the preserve, which includes part of the Black-Capped Vireo Preserve. Along the ridges farther downstream, houses are starting to creep into the skyline, as is happening in many of the wilder areas in Austin. As you continue west, you'll merge with the Easy Access Loop.

KEY AT-A-GLANCE INFORMATION

LENGTH: 2.5 miles
CONFIGURATION: Loop
DIFFICULTY: Moderate
SCENERY: Creeks, hills, and typical Hill Country vegetation
EXPOSURE: Moderate
TRAFFIC: Heavy–light, depending on time and trails
TRAIL SURFACE: Packed dirt
HIKING TIME: 2 hours
ACCESS: Fees are collected in a box at the trailhead, based on the honor system.
MAPS: Trail map and interpretive booklet available at entrance or online at www.wildbasin.org
FACILITIES: None
SPECIAL COMMENTS: Pets and bicycles are not allowed; see www.wildbasin.org.

Directions ⟶

Entrance is located off of Loop 360 South, west of downtown, south of the Austin Lake Bridge.

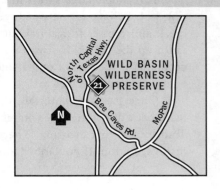

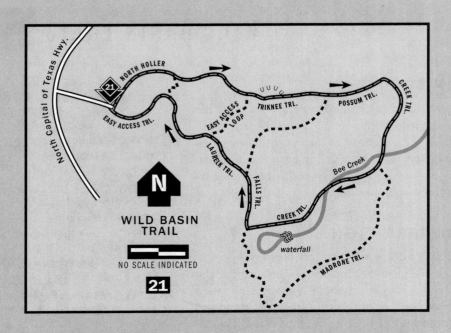

Shortly into the hike, you'll reach an area marked "overlook" on the trail map that offers some of the best vistas on this trail, including the creek that feeds Bee Creek. Numerous plaques offer information on the local bird life that you may encounter. The vegetation begins to thicken beyond this point as the trail descends toward Bee Creek. Though it's not too steep, caution is warranted in some places to ensure safe footing. You'll reach a side trail to the right, but keep going straight and work your way toward Bee Creek along the Triknee and Possum trails.

When you reach the fork in the trail, turn right. This is now the Creek Trail. When you reach the actual creek, you'll have to make the first of two crossings. There are ample large stones in the water that will allow you to cross without getting wet, as long as you watch your step. The trail continues to follow along the creek and crosses it again about 0.2 miles from the first crossing. An equal distance up the Creek Trail you'll find a waterfall on the left and a bench and outcropping of rock to sit on to your right. This is a good spot to take a break and enjoy an incredible view.

Once past the waterfall, the trail forks again. To the left, Madrone Trail leads back down the way you just came and eventually joins back with the Creek Trail by the first crossing. There is an interesting rock staircase and plenty of lush vegetation. If you aren't too tired by this point, explore this side trail, then follow the Creek Trail back up past the waterfall for a second look. Otherwise just take the Falls Trail to the right and start working your way back to the trailhead. You'll encounter one side trail on your right as you start the uphill hike. Keep going straight.

When the trail merges with the Easy Access Loop, you can go to the right to check out the interpretive areas that you missed on the way down, or keep going straight to go to the educational center and eventually your car. Regardless of which side trails you pick, chances are you won't see it all your first time and you'll want to make another trip to Wild Basin.

NORTH OF AUSTIN

22

BLUFFS OF THE NORTH FORK SAN GABRIEL RIVER

KEY AT-A-GLANCE INFORMATION

LENGTH: 4 miles

CONFIGURATION: Out-and-back

DIFFICULTY: Moderate

SCENERY: Lakeside woods and fields, bluffs

EXPOSURE: Mostly sunny

TRAFFIC: Moderate to busy on weekends

TRAIL SURFACE: Dirt, grass, rocks

HIKING TIME: 2.5 hours

ACCESS: Free

MAPS: None

FACILITIES: Water, restrooms at trailhead

IN BRIEF

This hike traces an old roadbed along the upper embayment of Lake Georgetown, passing bluffs of the North Fork San Gabriel River. It then opens to a flat before reaching more bluffs, where you can look up the river and beyond. From here, adventurous hikers will scramble up to the bluff line or into a nearby hollow.

DESCRIPTION

This hike encompasses part of the Good Water Hiking Trail, built by the U.S. Army Corps of Engineers. The trail encircles Lake Georgetown, then ties into city trails on its eastern end, making a trek of more than 20 miles around the lake. For this particular walk, leave Tejas Camp and head east on the Good Water Hiking Trail. The level walk leads past bluffs on the north side of the North Fork San Gabriel River and along flats to reach bluffs on the south side of Lake Georgetown, where you can overlook the impoundment and the land beyond.

Pick up the Good Water Hiking Trail by leaving the parking area and walking toward the low-water bridge over North Fork San

----

Directions ———————————→

From Austin, head north on Interstate 35 to Exit 261, Taylor/Burnet, TX 29. Head west on TX 29 to reach Sewards Junction, the intersection of TX 29 and US 183. From here, head north on US 183 and cross over the North Fork San Gabriel River. Just after the crossing, turn right onto TX 3405. Follow 3405 to CR 258. Turn right onto CR 258 to the low-water bridge crossing of the North Fork San Gabriel River. Tejas Camp is on the left just after the bridge. This hike starts on the south side, the Tejas Camp side, of the low-water bridge.

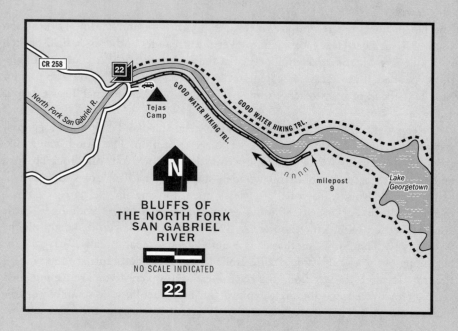

Gabriel River. Before crossing the bridge, look right for the path and begin following an old roadbed, passing Tejas Camp on your right. The North Fork San Gabriel River flows to your left. At this point, folks can be seen swimming, fishing, or tubing the river into the lake, where the waters are still. This area was historically known as the West End Crossing. It was the fourth upstream river crossing from Georgetown in pre-dam days. This is the only crossing between here and Georgetown that wasn't flooded by the lake. Hayden Hunt and his brothers settled at West End Crossing and built a log cabin, cotton gin, and corn mill. The bluffs across the river from Tejas Camp hold the family cemetery.

Occasional side trails leave left toward the river. At just over 0.5 miles, the aforementioned white and tan, cedar-studded bluffs tower over the river embayment. Along the trail, look for winged elm. This tree with an unusual name often grows in abandoned clearings. Winged elms are easily identified by their corky "wings" running along their branches. The fiberlike inner bark of this tree was made into rope and used to tie cotton bales in the 1800s.

Fields lie to your right. Bluffs rise in the distance. The Good Water Hiking Trail descends to a riverside flat, where a wet-weather stream comes in from the right. This streamlet and the entire San Gabriel drainage is part of the Brazos River system, which enters the Gulf of Mexico near Freeport, south of Houston.

The North Fork, where you are, meets the South Fork and Middle Fork of San Gabriel River near Georgetown. Step over the streamlet and cross a field broken by a lone live oak. Skirt around a fence at the end of the field to reach a double-track roadbed. Turn left here, staying on level land. Steep bluffs now rise to your right and ahead of you. Reach a stone post and sign indicating that Tejas Camp is 1.8 miles distant.

Keep forward, passing the mouth of the steep-sided and deep Jim Hogg Hollow to your right. This mini-canyon beckons exploration. The Good Water Hiking Trail keeps going forward, stepping over the outflow from Jim Hogg Hollow, and begins to ascend a bluff on wooden steps. The path narrows and tunnels beneath thick woods. To your left, views open, looking up the narrow embayment of North Fork San Gabriel River. Across the water is wide-open cattle country, settled with a few houses. As you keep forward, you'll shortly hit the 9-mile post. This indicates that it is 9 miles from Cedar Breaks Park and the beginning of the Good Water Hiking Trail. The post is a good turnaround point— the trail descends to flats along the river ahead. However, if you are feeling energetic, before you leave the area explore Jim Hogg Hollow or scramble up the bluffs above you. They flatten out and offer extensive views of the area.

CAMP CREEK TRAIL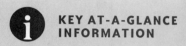

IN BRIEF

A hike more reminiscent of a walk down a country road than a trail in the hills, Camp Creek offers open prairies and hardwood stands for hikers and equestrians to enjoy the abundant wildlife that lives near Lake Travis. Mountain bikers will enjoy the wide trails to hone their skills negotiating the rocks.

DESCRIPTION

This park appears to have been forgotten by most, but a hike here will be very popular with families and individuals wanting an opportunity to see the area's wildlife in its natural habitat. The bulletin board in the parking lot has a topographical map of the area. The black-and-white map is difficult to read.

The trail is hard to discern from the road. To reach the trailhead, look for a sign (visible on the north side of the parking lot) that prohibits vehicular traffic. This is the beginning of the trail. At this point the trail is loose gravel with obvious ruts from maintenance trucks. Head up the trail (and the hill). There are a few red ant beds along the path, so wear your boots and watch your step. The wide and obvious path will allow you to see any hazards that might exist along the trail, including prints of horseback riders and mountain bikers.

KEY AT-A-GLANCE INFORMATION

LENGTH: 1.8 miles

CONFIGURATION: Balloon

DIFFICULTY: Easy

SCENERY: Grass prairies and hardwoods, numerous species of birds and wildlife

EXPOSURE: Open

TRAFFIC: Very light

TRAIL SURFACE: Rock, dirt, and gravel

HIKING TIME: 45 minutes

ACCESS: Open for day use; campsites are also available in area

MAPS: None

FACILITIES: None

SPECIAL COMMENTS: This area is maintained by the Lower Colorado River Authority (LCRA) and is not kept in prime condition. Boxes that claim to have maps in them are generally full of advertisements, if anything. The LCRA has no trail maps for this area.

Directions

From Austin, take FR 1431 west toward Marble Falls. Turn left on Shaw Road. From San Antonio, take US 281 to Marble Falls and turn right on FM 1431. Shaw Road is 9 miles east. Turn right. Follow Shaw Road to posted entrance signs, and follow until you reach a sign that reads TRAILHEAD. The trailhead is located on the opposite side of railing.

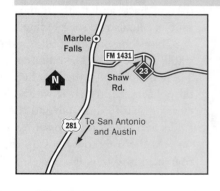

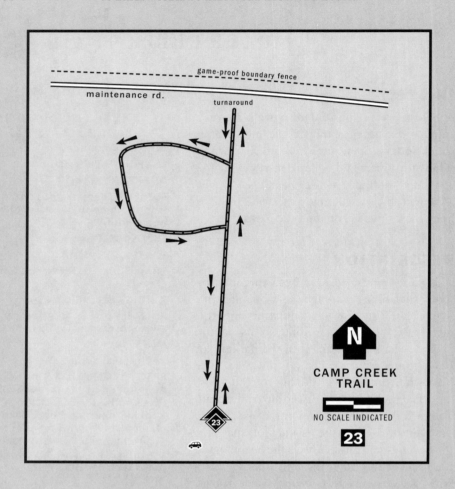

The first few hundred feet of the trail is lined with mesquite bushes and weeds, as well as prickly pear cactus. Watch the area for cardinals and blue jays darting back and forth in the brush. Eastern cottontails and black-tailed jackrabbits can also be seen hiding in the ground cover.

Not long into the trail is a dilapidated building that was probably a corral or stable at one time. The building is collapsed, and there is a partial fence around it. There is also a hitching post here that appears to get some use. The metal horizontal pole indicates that it was added more recently than the fallen structure. The clearing that lies just beyond the building off the trail looks like a good spot for riders and hikers alike to set up a picnic and enjoy a morning in the sun.

As the trail continues up the hill, the gravel gradually turns to dirt and the road begins to look less traveled. The ruts become parallel paths, passing stands of old-growth cedar and hackberry trees, as well as the occasional live oak and large mesquite.

For novice trackers, this road is a great place to hone their skills. Tracks and scat are seen easily in the dirt. Species indicated along the trail include the ever-present deer, as well as coyotes, javelina, armadillos, and rabbits. Coyotes in particular appear to make use of the trail. This is common among these lazy predators, who tend to make the best use of roads for quieter stalking and easier travel.

A half mile into the hike the path surface becomes dirt and demonstrates how little use the area gets. Grasses and weeds have taken root on the trail, only to be trampled by the occasional hiker. At just over 0.5 miles, there is a spur to the right (part of an old road system) then a second fork shortly ahead that leads to the left. For now, continue right, past the fork to reach a high, game-proof fence by a maintenance road. Deer and other wildlife in the woods across the boundary may show themselves to quiet hikers. Turn back at this point, and hike 0.1 mile back to the fork. Turn right. This path is just as wide as the beginning, but it looks less used.

You'll pass by fields in between stands of trees that offer great opportunities for watching deer in the morning and evenings. It's one thing to speed by them as you drive through the Hill Country, but it's a real treat to walk up to an open field where a group of bucks are sparring before the winter mating season begins. In the early summer, mothers stand guard while their fawns frolic.

Another fork appears to the left at nearly a mile, heading downhill. Take this fork, which shows even less use. Depending on the time of year and amount of rainfall, the trail surface may appear overgrown but can still be made out compared with the high grasses that surround it. At about 1.2 miles, the loop rejoins the main trail, where you will turn right to return to the trailhead. You'll again pass the old corral and hitching post and maybe even a horseback rider or two. When you do encounter horses, make your presence known well ahead of time so you don't spook the animals. Once the rider answers, be prepared to pass them on the left.

You'll reach the trailhead after hiking almost 2 miles and probably find that your car is still the only one in the parking lot. Though getting away from the crowds is great, the lack of use seems to cause a lack of maintenance of the area, or it could be the other way around. Regardless of reasons, this beautiful place is available to all and should be taken advantage of.

COMANCHE BLUFFS TRAIL

KEY AT-A-GLANCE INFORMATION

LENGTH: 2.4 miles

CONFIGURATION: Out-and-back

DIFFICULTY: Easy

SCENERY: Mostly wooded lakeshore

EXPOSURE: Mostly shady

TRAFFIC: Moderate in summer, very light in colder months

TRAIL SURFACE: Dirt single-track

HIKING TIME: 2 hours

ACCESS: Free

MAPS: At corps office on way in to trailhead

FACILITIES: Water fountain, restroom at trailhead

IN BRIEF

This hike travels along the shoreline of Granger Lake, an underutilized resource of central Texas. You'll hike through extremely thick forests, which thrive in the fertile soils of the Blackland Prairie. Two historic bridges, which spanned the now-flooded waters of the San Gabriel River, have been moved to the path.

DESCRIPTION

This trail will surprise most central Texans. Simply put, there are few areas that feature such dense woodland. The trail travels through lakeside thickets formed by hardwoods. The path also has open areas that overlook Granger Lake. Damming the San Gabriel River, which crosses the fertile Blackland Prairie, formed Granger Lake. The combination of moist surroundings and rich bottomland are reminiscent of Eastern forests.

Leave the trailhead, immediately descending on the Comanche Bluffs Trail. This is known as the east trailhead. Descend to quickly reach a seemingly out-of-place iron trestle bridge that far exceeds the dimensions of any normal trail bridge. This is a special bridge, for it is both historic and haunted.

- →

Directions —————————————————————→

From Austin, head north on I-35 to Exit 261, Taylor/Burnet, TX 29. Head east on TX 29 for 15.5 miles to reach TX 95 at a T intersection. Turn right, south on TX 95, and follow it 0.8 miles to Texas Ranch Road 1331, crossing the San Gabriel River. Turn left on 1331, toward Hare, and follow it 4.7 miles to Taylor Park. Turn left into Taylor Park and follow the main road past the entrance station 0.3 miles to the side road leading a short distance left to the trailhead.

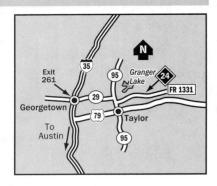

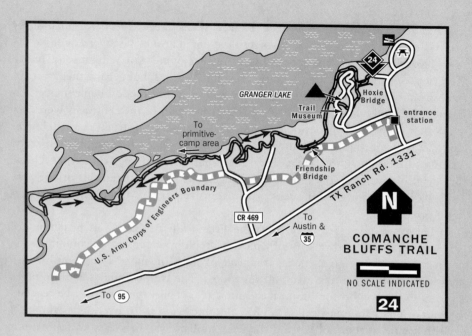

The Hoxie Bridge was erected 3.5 miles east of Circleville around 1900, spanning the San Gabriel River where Granger Lake lies today.

During the devastating 1921 flood, the Hoxie Bridge was washed 300 yards downstream. In November of that year, a firm was awarded the contract to restore the bridge. A team of convict laborers was sent from Huntsville to aid in the reconstruction. One of the hardened prisoners was a troublemaker. A guard made an example of him, shooting him in the head and hanging him in a nearby tree at the work site, as a grisly reminder to keep the prisoners in line. The bridge was finished and life returned to normal in Circleville. After some time, residents and passersby began to report that the bottomland around the bridge was patrolled by a headless ghost on Friday nights during a full moon. A priest was brought in to pray for the convict's soul and allegedly ended the haunting. In 1979, the bridge was removed from the river before flooding of the lake and was repositioned here by the Army Corps of Engineers. Moving the bridge may have stirred the wrath of the convict ghost, so keep an eye out Friday nights during a full moon.

Ahead, uphill, is the recreation area campground. The Comanche Bluffs Trail veers right and circles the campground. Granger Lake is to your right. Soon you reach the shoreline and pass several cross-trails connecting the lake to the campground, while keeping west in dense hardwoods. The single-track path works up little hills and down wet-weather drainages.

Climb away from the lake at nearly 1 mile, out to grass and cactus. A final trail from the campground merges with the Comanche Bluffs Trail. Shortly you'll reach the Friendship Bridge. It once spanned Willis Creek, a feeder branch of the San Gabriel River, which now flows into the north arm of Granger Lake.

Bridges like this were important to the development of Williamson County. The rich soils of the Blackland Prairie grew fertile crops, but getting them to market was another matter. The deep stream channels and muddy banks made permanent bridge building difficult until the 1880s. Before then, bridges were low and often swept away by periodic floods. The stronger iron structures with higher abutments made the bridges more reliable. The improved transportation made getting to markets more viable. The same flood of 1921 that ruined the Hoxie Bridge also devastated the Friendship Bridge. The Corps moved this bridge here as well. Today, prairie wildflowers grow extensively in this former farmland during April and May.

Leave to the right, away from the Friendship Bridge, shortly spanning a stream on a long boardwalk. Briefly pick up an old roadbed before climbing away from the lake to reach the west trailhead of the Comanche Bluffs Trail at 1.2 miles. Here are a parking area and restrooms. The trail continues 3 more miles beyond to the Fox Bottom Primitive Camp Area. (This camp can only be reached by foot or boat. You must call (512) 859-2668 to register for overnight camping.) The first mile of the trail beyond the west trailhead is fairly easy to follow, but then it gets difficult as it winds through thick woods (where driftwood obliterates the trail) and across open prairies (where numerous deer, horse, and foot trails merge and become confusing). Do not continue unless you are an experienced hiker with plenty of daylight to roam. Boardwalks span many of the feeder branches leading into Granger Lake. Parts of the trail are directly along the lake. Otherwise, turn back and enjoy the first portion of the trail a second time. You may want to cut through the campground and check out the Trail Museum, located in the Taylor Park Campground across from campsite #36.

CROCKETT GARDENS AND FALLS

IN BRIEF

This is one of the most unsung and best hikes in the Austin–San Antonio area. After tunneling through dense woods, it opens onto tall bluffs overlooking Lake Georgetown. From there, you'll circle around a stream to reach Crockett Gardens and Falls. Here, a crystalline spring emanates from a rock ridge, then tumbles over a bluff overgrown with vegetation alongside the falls.

DESCRIPTION

This walk was surprising and a hit from beginning to end and back! The hike encompasses a section of the Good Water Hiking Trail, which makes a circuit of Lake Georgetown on U.S. Army Corps of Engineers and city of Georgetown land. The rich cedar woods make for shady hiking, then sheer 100-foot bluffs open up vistas extending the length of Lake Georgetown. Beyond that point, the trail circles a stream to reach an old homesite and Crockett Gardens and Falls. The springhead flows a short distance to tumble over an unlikely bluff into Lake Georgetown. The rich vegetation around the spring run and falls is attractive and makes a great picnic locale.

Leave the large trailhead on a gravel path extending into cedar woods. At almost

KEY AT-A-GLANCE INFORMATION

LENGTH: 5 miles
CONFIGURATION: Out-and-back
DIFFICULTY: Moderate
SCENERY: Cedar woods, lake bluffs, springs
EXPOSURE: Half sunny, half shady
TRAFFIC: Moderate–busy on weekends
TRAIL SURFACE: Rock, dirt
HIKING TIME: 3.5 hours, including lunch at springs
ACCESS: Free
MAPS: Available at park
FACILITIES: Restrooms, water at park picnic area

Directions ———————————————➤

From Exit 261A on I-35, Lake Georgetown/ Andice, take Texas Ranch Road 2338 west. Travel west for 3.3 miles, then turn left onto Cedar Breaks Road. Follow Cedar Breaks Road west for 2.1 miles, crossing the Lake Georgetown Dam along the way to reach the Cedar Breaks Park entrance station. Take the first left beyond the entrance station and reach the trailhead.

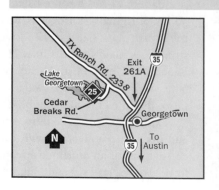

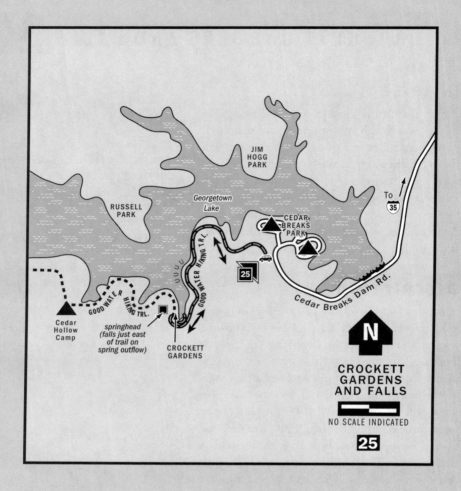

CROCKETT
GARDENS
AND FALLS

NO SCALE INDICATED

25

0.5 miles, cross a small, rocky ravine. The gravel has given way to rocks and dirt. Ahead, reach a stone marker. This is Second Booty's Crossing, which in pre-dam days was a route used by travelers up the North Fork San Gabriel River Valley. Originally known as Russell Crossing, this was the second crossing of the North Fork San Gabriel River above Georgetown. The trail of gnarly limestone now makes a bluff line. Here, you can look across the lake at Russell Park. Reach the 1-mile post. Ahead, more views open up, extending the length of the lake. Walk to the bluff's edge—some of the drops are sheer and 100 feet or more down to the alluring blue water.

Continue along the bluff, gaining more views. Pass through an old wire fence and open into a clearing with cactus, rock, and grass. Begin to circle around the embayment of an unnamed stream, passing the 2-mile post. Dip into the sycamore-lined stream, quickly climbing out and to a clearing, where stone relics of an old homestead stand near a cedar-post corral in varied stages of decay. Bisect the corral and reach a trail sign at 2.4 miles. Ahead is Crockett Spring, but turn right here toward the base of the falls. Jump over the streambed below and work around the lake's edge on an old roadbed that now leads into the lake. You'll begin to hear falling water. Across the embayment is Crockett Falls. You can see the narrow stream stair-stepping down a bluff. Lush vegetation lines the falls on its descent.

Return to the main trail and reach the spring run and upper falls. Many a settler has coveted this area. It went through several hands until James Knight operated a flour mill and grew fruits and vegetables in the area, including the first strawberries in Williamson County. Later, R. M. Crockett, who gave the area its name, operated a truck garden. Crockett grew produce and took it to Austin to sell. On the far side of the fence, outside Army Corps of Engineers property, you can see concrete foundations and outlines of buildings, as well as the stone house and corral relics nearby. Large pecan trees shade the spring run and benches. The outflow of the spring is visible near the base of a low rock ridge. The falls from above are quite a sight, too. It is easy to see why this is one of the most coveted spots in central Texas.

NEARBY ACTIVITIES

Cedar Breaks Park has a picnic area, campground, and boat landing. For more information, call (512) 930-LAKE.

26   RIM ROCK LOOP AT DOESKIN RANCH

KEY AT-A-GLANCE INFORMATION

LENGTH: 3 miles

CONFIGURATION: Loop

DIFFICULTY: Moderate

SCENERY: Riparian creek, prairie, open plateau

EXPOSURE: Mostly sunny

TRAFFIC: Little to moderate

TRAIL SURFACE: Dirt, grass, rocks

HIKING TIME: 1.5 hours

ACCESS: Free

MAPS: None available

FACILITIES: Restroom at trailhead

IN BRIEF

This relatively new trail system is a little-known hiking gem. A set of trails has been established in this unit of the Balcones Canyonlands National Wildlife Refuge at the old Doeskin Ranch. This unit of the refuge, northwest of Austin, travels through prime golden-cheeked warbler habitat, first along a creek then through open grasslands and up to a plateau, where Hill Country views await. A short side hike includes a serene pond.

DESCRIPTION

This little getaway will leave you wishing there were more trails to hike here. But the loop described will have to suffice. Leave the trailhead and circle around a feeder branch of Cow Creek. Climb through grassland to reach a plateau where views of Texas Hill Country await. Circle back down, enjoying a bit more creekside canyon scenery before completing your loop.

This hike travels through prime golden-cheeked warbler habitat. This bird, which lives only in central Texas, is the primary reason for the establishment of the Balcones Canyonlands National Wildlife Preserve, which preserves other species while conserving the warbler habitat. When Spanish explorers named the layers of hills northwest of Austin "Balcones,"

Directions

From Austin, take US 183 north into the town of Cedar Park. Turn left on RR 1431 and follow it west for 26 miles to Texas Ranch Road 1174. Turn right and head north on RR 1174, following it for 4.6 miles. Look right for the Doeskin Ranch. There will also be a sign indicating that this is part of the Balcones Canyonlands National Wildlife Refuge. A short paved path leads down to the main trailhead.

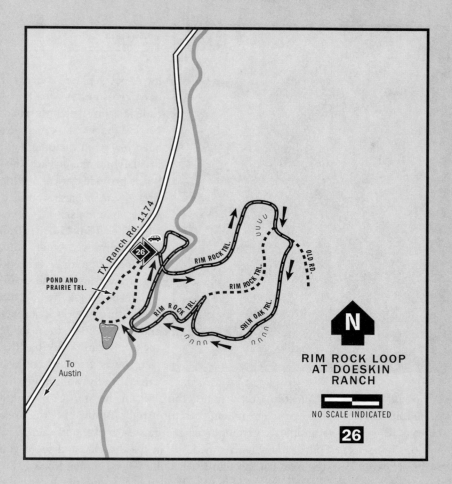

they had no idea their name would carry through the ages. But these limestone hills and spring-fed canyons are a treasure worth preserving.

Doeskin Ranch is just one unit of the Balcones Canyonlands National Wild-life Refuge. Other units are scattered in the hills south. Start your Doeskin Ranch exploration by taking the Creek Trail past a wooden crib left from the days when this was a working ranch. Curve past a stone fence, another relic of the past, then work down toward the unnamed feeder branch of Cow Creek. Cypress and syca-more trees line the water course. Large boulders lying in the creek have fallen from the limestone walls. The path skirts the divide between creekside woodland and grassland. Follow this perimeter to meet the Rim Rock Trail at just over 0.5 miles. Turn left here, following the roadbed. (The single-track Rim Rock Trail ahead of you is your return route.) Shortly you'll cross the creek. Stepping stones

have been placed here for easy crossing. A small cascade falls just below the road. Notice the bat box that has been placed in the open land just beyond the stream. The boxes provide critical nesting sites for these insect-eating mammals.

The Rim Rock Trail angles through open land, heading for a draw. Ascend the draw, leaving the road-bed. The single-track path winds through thick juniper and oak woods to reach a rocky plateau. Look back to gain views from where you came. Briefly walk along the plateau and reach a trail junction at 1.3 miles. Turn left on the Shin Oak Trail, a roadbed. It cuts across the open plateau and then turns right. Amble over the open country with successive junipers emerging from the grasses, rocks, and cacti. The vistas of the adjacent Hill Country are many. Look in the distance and see if you can spot Hickory Pass, the road cut through Tater Hill on Texas Ranch Road 1174, the auto route to Doeskin Ranch. The Shin Oak Trail curves around the edge of the plateau to reach the Rim Rock Trail at 1.8 miles. Turn left here, dipping off the plateau on a single-track path. Many switchbacks ease the descent. The trailhead is easily visible below. The woods give way to grassland, briefly broken by a live oak grove. Keep descending to reach the creek again. Stepping stones make this crossing easy, too. Head upstream, passing a side branch flowing out of the nearby pond. Shortly you'll reach the end of the Rim Rock Trail and turn left, returning to the trailhead at 2.6 miles. Before you leave, however, take the time to walk the nearly half-mile Pond and Prairie Trail, which overlooks a stock pond and the creek. Contemplation benches have been placed along the pathway.

NEARBY ACTIVITIES

Balcones Canyonlands National Wildlife Refuge is made up of many units. Birdwatching, hunting, and hiking are the primary activities on the system. For more information, call (512) 339-9432 or visit **www.fws.gov/southwest/refuges/texas/balcones/index.htm**.

SOUTHEAST OF AUSTIN

27   BUESCHER HIKING TRAIL

KEY AT-A-GLANCE INFORMATION

LENGTH: 4.2 miles

CONFIGURATION: Balloon

DIFFICULTY: Moderate

SCENERY: Pine woods

EXPOSURE: More shade than sun

TRAFFIC: Light to moderate

TRAIL SURFACE: Leaves, pine needles, dirt, some rocks

HIKING TIME: 2.25 hours

ACCESS: $4/person park-entrance fee

MAPS: Available at park office and online at www.tpwd.state.tx.us/spdest/findadest/parks/buescher

FACILITIES: Water, restroom at picnic area

IN BRIEF

This trail circles through the western end of the Lost Pines, an outlier stand of loblolly pines reminiscent of the piney woods of east Texas. At Buescher State Park, the pine woods are located on both level land and in deep ravines, adding ups and down to this loop.

DESCRIPTION

This is an underhiked trail in an underutilized state park. Hikers should consider incorporating other activities, such as camping, swimming, and fishing, into a trip here. Nearby Bastrop State Park gets most of the action in these parts, though Buescher has good scenery as well. Both share a slice of the Lost Pines, a stretch of loblolly pine forest much like that in east Texas. The Buescher Hiking Trail travels exclusively amid the Lost Pines, where yaupon

----

Directions

From the junction of US 183 and TX 71 near the Austin airport, take TX 71 east for 35 miles to the TX 95 South/Loop 230, Smithville/Flatonia exit. Get off the divided highway and turn left onto FR 153 (which is not listed on the exit sign off TX 71). Turn left and head north for 0.6 miles to the Buescher State Park entrance. Pass the park entrance, and stay on Park Road 1. After 0.8 miles, you will see the Buescher Hiking Trail trailhead on your right. Do not start here. Instead, drive just a short distance farther, then turn right onto Park Road 1C. Follow Park Road 1C for 1.7 miles to the entrance of the University of Texas Science Park. A parking area is on the left just beyond the entrance to the science park. Pick up the Buescher Hiking Trail as it crosses the road to the science park, heading northeast, the same side as the parking area, and away from the state park entrance.

To Austin

71

BUESCHER STATE PARK

FR 153

N

95 **71**

Smithville

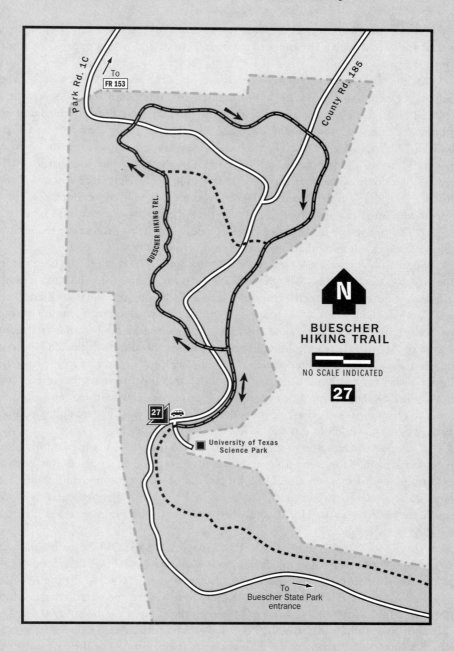

N

BUESCHER
HIKING TRAIL

NO SCALE INDICATED

27

Park Rd. 1C

To
FR 153

County Rd. 185

BUESCHER HIKING TRL.

27

University of Texas
Science Park

To
Buescher State Park
entrance

and oaks complement the tall evergreens that reach for the sky. Desiccated ravines break the terrain where the pines grow their richest, and hikers experience some vertical variation.

Pick up the Buescher Hiking Trail as it crosses the Science Center Road. The walking is easy and level amid loblolly pines, live oaks, and red oaks. Copper-colored rocks dot the trailbed. On the way in you may have noticed the elaborate stonework done on park buildings and shelters. The Civilian Conservation Corps built these back in the 1930s. The rock slabs were cut from this very same rock. A few buildings of the science center are visible off the path. The single-track path reaches the loop portion of the hike at 0.4 miles. Turn left here to cross Park Road 1C. A shady mix of woods darkens the path as you curve along a ravine. Shortly dip into the gulch. Notice the forest is richer here—the oaks and pines are bigger. The ravine collects and preserves moisture and helps protect the trees from temperature extremes, enhancing the growing environment.

Span a small ravine on a boardwalk, then climb to level land. The contrast in the two forests is evident. The plateau area is more exposed to the sun's drying influence and is more open. The trees are smaller and somewhat stunted. The walk on level land doesn't last long—the trail begins working into another ravine before reaching a shortcut trail at 1.4 miles. The shortcut leads just over 0.5 miles across the loop. The main path is littered with pine needles as it descends into a bigger ravine, known as Pine Gulch. You may see pools of water in the base of Pine Gulch or even flow in the cooler months or following rains. Begin cruising down Pine Gulch, a beautiful little valley that exudes a wilderness aura. Before long, the trail dips to the base of the gulch and crosses over the streambed. Climb away from Pine Gulch to cross Park Road 1C at 1.8 miles.

Continue to enjoy the fragrant pine woods. A nickname for the loblolly pine is "rosemary pine" for its fragrant and resinous foliage. In other places it is known as "bull pine" for its giant size. Loblolly pine is the major commercial pine in the Southeastern states. It is extensively cultivated. Its natural range extends from southern New Jersey to Florida and west to Texas. The pines here are at their most westerly range.

Travel over small, undulating hills to reach CR 185, Old Antioch Road, at 2.6 miles. The Buescher Hiking Trail travels alongside a shallow streambed. Parts of the forest open up as you reach an old dirt road at 3.1 miles. To the left is a gated private road. Here the trail splits. Stay left, toward the gated entrance but not through it, as the trail leaving right is the other end of the just over 0.5 miles shortcut. Keep winding through the woods and come across a dammed pond. Reach a final trail junction at 3.8 miles. This is the beginning of the loop portion of the path. Keep forward this time and backtrack nearly 0.5 miles to complete the hike.

Loblolly-pine forest

NEARBY ACTIVITIES

This state park offers camping and fishing as well as hiking. For more information, call (512) 237-2241, or visit **www.tpwd.state.tx.us/spdest/findadest/ parks/buescher.**

28   LOCKHART STATE PARK TRAIL

KEY AT-A-GLANCE INFORMATION

LENGTH: 0.7 miles

CONFIGURATION: Loop

DIFFICULTY: Easy

SCENERY: Hardwoods

EXPOSURE: Shady

TRAFFIC: Very light

TRAIL SURFACE: Dirt

HIKING TIME: 30 minutes

ACCESS: Open to day use; $2 entry fee is waived for Conservation Passport holders

MAPS: None

FACILITIES: Restrooms, vending machines, swimming pool, 9-hole golf course

IN BRIEF

Enjoy the birds and wildlife on this short jaunt around the south side of Lockhart State Park. This is a great walk to take the kids on before heading over to the swimming pool or enjoying a round of golf on the only Texas Parks and Wildlife–run golf course.

DESCRIPTION

When the Great Depression had the nation in a state of despair, young men joined President Franklin D. Roosevelt's Civilian Conservation Corps (CCC) with the hope of making a living and maybe a difference. Of the more than 1,400 works camps in the nation, 15 were located in Texas, and they were responsible for a great number of the state-park and forest facilities still in use today. Lockhart State Park is one of those places that benefited from their presence.

Men working for anything from $30 to $40 a month built numerous buildings, roads, and dams across the state. In Lockhart, they constructed a swimming pool alongside Plum Creek that utilizes the spring water, and a bridge over the creek that adds to the aesthetic qualities of the park. The park work was complete in 1938, but it wasn't used as a state park until 1948. In that interim period it was leased to a nearby country club.

The trailhead is located near a small bridge/dam of Clear Fork Creek. Here, the water trickles at a leisurely pace, and golfers

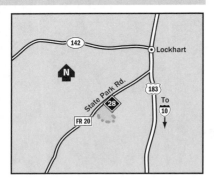

Directions

To reach the park, go 1 mile south of Lockhart on US 183 to FM 20, then southwest on FM 20 for 2 miles to Park Road 10, then 1 mile south on Park Road 10.

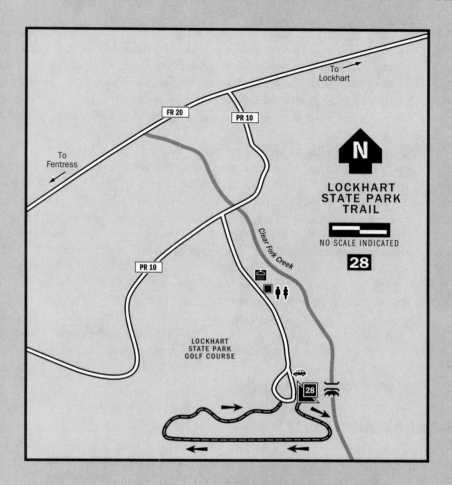

often take a break to wet a fishing line from their golf carts. To the right of the creek, you can see the trail leading into the trees under a thick, shady canopy. This little-used trail looks inviting and could very well have inspired Robert Frost's poem "The Road Not Taken," had he lived in Texas instead of New England. Even in the summer there is a bed of leaves on the otherwise dirt trail, which is wide enough to allow two or more to walk abreast. The light through the tree-tops creates shadows that dance on the trail surface. As you start down the trail, Clear Fork Creek can be seen to the left. In the morning, nutria can be seen swimming back and forth in its clear waters, and turtles lounge around all day long. To the right, the dense woods hide foxes, deer, and rabbits, as well as numerous species of songbirds.

About halfway into the hike, you will reach a fence. Turn right and walk beside it for a while. The forested area gives way to grassland that falls victim to the occasional controlled burn, which is sometimes evident, either by charred ground or very new growth. After following the fence for about 200 yards, the trail cuts to the right back into the woods and narrows to allow only one hiker at a time. The trees and ground cover crowd the trail, and the incline gains about 50 feet over the next 0.2 miles.

Songbirds remind hikers of their presence vocally, but they are rarely seen in the thick woods. Fallen trees scattered to the sides of the path show the age of the flora in the park, which has probably never been cultivated. The oaks and cedars have stood undisturbed for centuries. Keep an eye out for spider webs crossing the trail. Because the trail sees little use, resident arachnids—some of which grow to a pretty remarkable size—can build some very intricate traps. The thick ground growth also serves as inviting habitat to scorpions, snakes, and tarantulas. Though not as big as the ones seen in the movies or the National Geographic specials, these hairy spiders are big enough that you'll want to avoid them. Chances are if you do see one, it will be darting or jumping out of your way.

When the trail turns to the right again it widens back to its original size. This very gentle slope leads back down toward the parking lot, but not before affording you the opportunity to watch cardinals and doves cross the trail above, and lizards a rabbits cross it below. Another 0.3 miles and the trail ends in the parking area, less than 50 yards from where it began.

NEARBY ACTIVITIES

If you have the time and your golf clubs, you can squeeze in a round of golf. You could also head over to the spring-fed swimming hole. You could head south to the Palmetto State Park to enjoy the trails there, which are included in this book. If you drive that way, stop in Luling for some of the best barbecue around.

LOST PINES HIKING TRAIL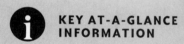

IN BRIEF

The Lost Pines Hiking Trail is an outstanding path. It offers an attractive, lengthy loop in a wooded setting in which backpacking is a possibility. Forested valleys, mini-gorges, and wood ravines divide pine- and oak-covered hills. The trail is both well marked and well maintained.

DESCRIPTION

The Lost Pines Hiking Trail starts across Park Road 1A from the stone gazebo. Immediately descend into tall loblolly pines—their needles drop onto the understory vegetation and carpet the forest floor a rusty red. The trailbed becomes sandy and the forest opens before reaching Overlook Junction at almost 0.5 miles. Veer left here as the trailbed narrows to a single-track footpath winding amid small clearings and through scattered pine belts and oak domes.

By now you have noticed the metal rectangular markers nailed to trees at eye level. Their position indicates the direction the trail travels. At 0.7 miles, cross the Old Road Bed. This former road divides the area. Backcountry camping is allowed beyond this point. However, ground fires are prohibited. The

KEY AT-A-GLANCE INFORMATION

LENGTH: 8.1 miles
CONFIGURATION: Loop
DIFFICULTY: Moderate–difficult
SCENERY: Pine woods, creek bottoms
EXPOSURE: Mostly shady
TRAFFIC: Moderate
TRAIL SURFACE: Pines needles, leaves, dirt, sand
HIKING TIME: 4.75 hours
ACCESS: $4 park-entrance fee
MAPS: At park or online at www .tpwd.state.tx.us/spdest/findadest/ parks/bastrop
FACILITIES: Water, picnic table, restrooms in day-use area near park pool

Directions

From the Austin airport, head east on TX 71 for 25 miles to TX 95 in Bastrop. Turn left and drive north on TX 95 for 0.4 miles to TX 21. Turn right and head east on TX 21 to reach Bastrop State Park. Pass the park entrance station, then turn left on Park Road 1A and follow it for 1.2 miles to the trailhead, on your right. The Lost Pines Hiking Trail starts on the far side of the road from the stone gazebo at the parking area.

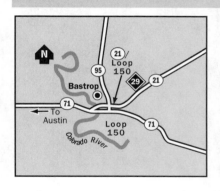

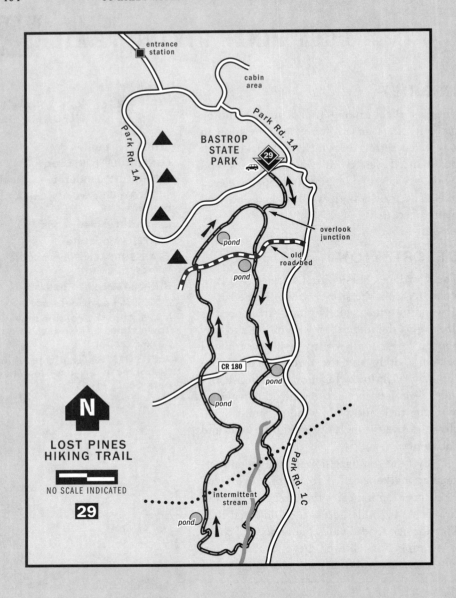

Lost Pines Hiking Trail then ascends a hill past an old fence line. The hill is rich with loblolly pines.

Reach County Road 180 at just over 1.5 miles. Cross the dirt road. Ahead, the trail passes over the dam of a pond. Soon pick up a straight, wide roadbed that contrasts with the winding nature of the path so far. The trail shortly leaves the roadbed and melds with the rounded shapes of nature: an old pine log, the bough of a cedar tree, and smooth creek pebbles.

The trail begins to skirt the north edge of a creek valley. The unnamed creek feeds Alum Creek. Views can be had into the creek valley. A multitude of green shades are seen below: bright green pine needles, darker green cedar trees, duller green oak leaves, and lighter yaupon leaves. Their fallen comrades color the ground with varying shades of brown. Drop into the valley, passing an unusual bent oak tree that could be used as a seat, then reach the unnamed creek at mile 3. The trail crosses the water course. This is the first of numerous crossings. These creek crossings are easy except in times of flood, when you shouldn't be on this trail at all. Notice the little bluffs the creek has cut into the hillsides. The Lost Pines Hiking Trail crosses a power-line cut, then returns along the streambed to make a trail junction at mile 3.8. This is known as Buescher Junction. At some point a trail will leave left to connect Bastrop State Park with nearby Buescher State Park.

For now, stay right with the Lost Pines Hiking Trail and cross the creek one last time for good measure. The path climbs and curves back to the northwest, crossing the power-line cut for a second time, then coming to another pond. This clear pond is fed by a small streamlet. These ponds are good habitat for the Houston toad, with a known realm of nine Texas counties. The toad's best habitat is here at this state park. The 3,000 to 4,000 remaining amphibians are active year-round but burrow to escape extreme heat and cold. They live on insects, such as ants. Keep along the watercourse, heading upstream. Pass another pond shortly before reaching CR 180 at mile 6. Traverse the dirt road and top a hill, dropping into mostly lush woods. Keep an eye out for some of the largest loblolly pines along the trail just before again crossing the Old Road Bed to leave the backcountry camping area of the trail.

Look for a rock outcrop on the trail left just before reaching Trailhead Junction at mile 7.1. Turn right on a sandy track, heading toward Overlook Junction. The trees stay tall as you reach a pretty pond. Pines ring the coffee-colored water. The woods open up some before reaching Overlook Junction at 7.7 miles. You've been here before. Turn left onto the sandy track and make your way nearly 0.5 miles back to the trailhead, digging deep for that last bit of energy on the final climb.

NEARBY ACTIVITIES

Bastrop State Park has two good campgrounds, cabins, and picnic areas and is near the historic town of Bastrop. A 13-mile scenic drive connects Bastrop State Park with Buescher State Park to the east. For more information, call (800) 792-1112 or visit **www.tpwd.state.tx.us/spdest/findadest/parks/bastrop.**

30 MONUMENT HILL HISTORY AND NATURE WALK

KEY AT-A-GLANCE INFORMATION

LENGTH: 1.25 miles

CONFIGURATION: Figure-8

DIFFICULTY: Easy

SCENERY: River bluff, sculpted lawn, oak woods

EXPOSURE: Mostly shady

TRAFFIC: Moderate on weekends

TRAIL SURFACE: Wood, rock, gravel, sidewalk

HIKING TIME: 1 hour

ACCESS: $2 access fee

MAPS: Online at www.tpwd.state.tx .us/park/monument

FACILITIES: Picnic area, restrooms

IN BRIEF

This hike showcases the site of Texas independence heroes' tomb, a pioneer's house, and brewery, all set on a bluff offering extensive views into the Colorado River Valley. Come on weekends and enjoy guided walks.

DESCRIPTION

Have you heard of the Black Bean Incident? Back when Texas was fighting for independence from Mexico in 1842, a group of militiamen from nearby La Grange went to battle with members of the Mexican army, led by General Adrian Woll, who had captured San Antonio. Woll routed the militia at Salado Creek. A group of Texans crossed into Mexico in retaliation, but most were captured by the Mexican army and forced to march toward Mexico City. Some escaped from the march but were soon recaptured. Following the escape, President Santa Anna ordered every tenth Texan executed. One hundred seventy-six beans were put in a pot, 17 of which were black. Each Texan was ordered to pull a bean. Those who plucked one of the black beans were executed on March 23, 1844.

In 1847, a survivor who plucked a white bean, John Duesenberry, led the retrieval of the executed. The remains, along with those who

----

Directions

From Austin, take TX 71 east to TX Business 71 near La Grange. Turn right onto TX Business 71 and follow it east 2.2 miles to US 77. Turn right, and head south on US 77 for 1.6 miles to TX Spur 92. Turn right on TX Spur 92 and follow it 0.4 miles to the park, on your right.

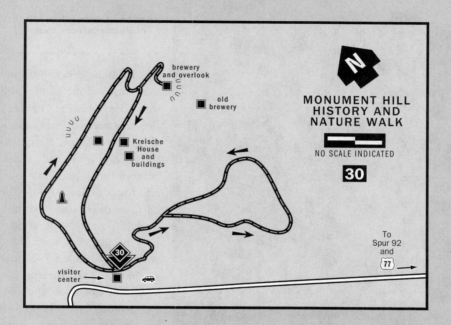

brewery
and overlook

old
brewery

MONUMENT HILL
HISTORY AND
NATURE WALK

NO SCALE INDICATED

30

Kreische
House
and
buildings

visitor
center

To
Spur 92
and
77

had battled Woll in 1842 at Salado Creek, were buried on what is known as Monument Hill, in 1848. Later, a tomb and monument were built, memorializing those who sacrificed their lives for Texas independence. This state park was established in 1983, after additional lands were acquired, including the home and brewery of Heinrich Kreische, all located on a bluff overlooking the Colorado River Valley and the town of La Grange below.

Leave the visitor center and meander through the well-manicured, oak-studded lawn along the Interpretive Trail with explanatory signage. Shortly reach the monument and interment location of the Texas heroes. On first glance it is hard to believe the grounds were severely neglected before it became a state park. Pass the monument to reach an escarpment overlooking the Colorado River and the town of La Grange. The Heinrich Kreische house is set back just a bit from the bluff line. Tours of the home are available on some Sundays. Check ahead with the park if you want to join a tour. The Interpretive Trail now heads along the bluff line to reach more stunning vistas looking northward. A long-range telescope allows you to gain closer views.

Turn away from the bluff and come to a side trail to another view. This one looks down into the ruins of Kreische's brewery in a small oak- and cedar-studded valley beside a small spring-fed stream below. You can see the elaborate rock work

View of the Colorado River

by Kreische incorporating the natural slope of the land into the brewing process. Brewery tours are also available on weekends. Return to the main trail and cruise behind the house and outbuildings. Check out the barn, smokehouse, and millstone. You may well wonder how he got any work done with such a fine vista so close at hand. The Interpretive Trail leads back to the visitor center, which has more information inside. Now, trace the Nature Trail as it makes a small loop into the upper part of the spring valley. Signposts indicate interesting flora of the landscape. Check with the park rangers for corresponding literature that explains the natural side of this historic spot.

PALMETTO STATE PARK TRAIL

IN BRIEF

The park's longest trail contains a mixture of hardwoods and palmettos that create an interesting and attractive ecosystem, which should be walked slowly to appreciate its diversity. This narrow, intimate hike passes several sights not normally seen along Hill Country trails.

DESCRIPTION

Lush would be the best way to begin describing this hike. Once off the park road, the foliage quickly crowds around the trail. This creates a canopy of shade that will stay with you for the remainder of the hike.

Two things to be aware of on this hike are snakes and spiders. Though it should be obvious to any hiker that snakes could be in the area, one should be especially cautious when the park officials actually go to the trouble of putting up signs to remind you. Although spiders are unlikely to pounce on you as you walk the trail, be on the lookout for webs that span the path.

Near the beginning of the trail, less than 50 yards from the road, there is an old wagon wheel on the ground that has been here for quite some time. It's been there so long, in fact, that a tree has grown around it. Parts of the rim of the wheel go right through the tree,

KEY AT-A-GLANCE INFORMATION

LENGTH: 1.5 miles

CONFIGURATION: Balloon

DIFFICULTY: Moderate

SCENERY: Palmettos, marsh, and lagoons

EXPOSURE: Shady

TRAFFIC: Light

TRAIL SURFACE: Dirt

HIKING TIME: 45 minutes

ACCESS: Open to day use 8 a.m.–10 p.m.; $3 entrance fee. Texas Conservation Passport holders are exempt from fees.

MAPS: Park maps are available at park headquarters for free or online at www.texasoutside.com/central texas/palmettostatepark.htm.

FACILITIES: Indoor toilets with showers, picnic tables, and playground

SPECIAL COMMENTS: Snakes may be present at certain times of year; watch for posted warning signs. Long pants and boots are a must for this hike. Walk slowly to take advantage of its aesthetic qualities. Average hiking time should be about 45 minutes, but take longer if you can.

Directions

From Luling, go east on US 183 onto Park Road 11. Park headquarters is about 2 miles down the road. After stopping for your map and to pay entrance fees, continue on the park road and take the second left after the office. Follow the road to a fork and turn left. This is the day-use parking area. Walk toward the camping areas where the road forked. The trail is on the right and clearly marked "Hiking Trail."

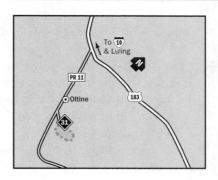

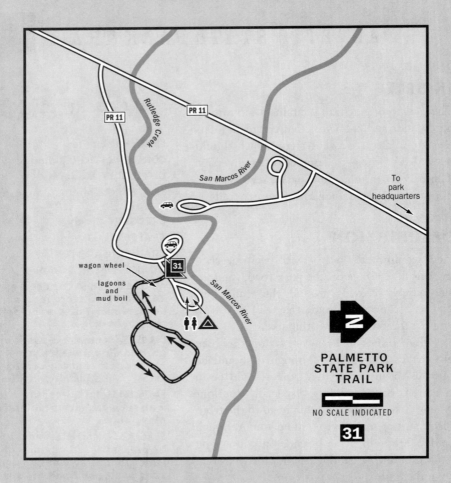

which doesn't seem to be otherwise affected. Be sure to look on the left side of the trail for this oddity.

Aside from the fact that there is a wagon wheel growing through the tree, you have to wonder not only how it got there but how it went unnoticed so long that a tree would have the time to grow around it. This has to be more than 100 years old. To the historically minded, it's easy to imagine that the Texas army lost it during the revolution against Mexico as they made their way toward San Jacinto for their final showdown with Santa Anna and his army.

As the trail meanders into the woods, you'll notice something else not often seen in this area of Texas—lagoons. There are two artesian wells located nearby that provide water to numerous small lagoons and swamps among the forest.

These moist conditions help provide the tropical feel of this trail by making the environment right for the dwarf palmetto plant, after which the park is named. A common sight in east Texas, the palmetto seems out of place here in the Hill Country yet thrives in this locale.

The first small water body is marked by a sign that designates it as the location of mud boils—warm springs that seem to have dried up, a phenomenon that hasn't occurred since the 1970s. The insect life is abundant all along the trail, but especially near the pools, which shrink in size during the summer months. Once you've passed this pond the canopy tightens, the hike becomes very shady, and the trail narrows because of the encroaching vegetation.

As the trail forks, you'll see a draw to your right that is worth stopping and witnessing. Full of palmettos and hardwoods, it is a mixture of the temperate and tropical zones that makes this hike unique. Continue following the trail to the right, and you'll find the only elevation on this hike. The trail dips down about six feet and levels right back out. Fallen leaves, butterflies, and grasshoppers mark the way, and it becomes difficult to walk two abreast from here to the end. At times there are so many grasshoppers that it sounds like you're walking through a popcorn popper. One could easily identify 20 or more species of butterfly along this section of the hike. The thick tree growth is also home to numerous species of birds, so take the time to scan the treetops for a tufted titmouse or prothonotary warbler.

The seclusion you experience on this trail is so engrossing that you'll find yourself approaching each turn with a feeling of not wanting it to end. Don't worry, because it doesn't end too soon. The sounds of armadillos rustling in the grass and the dancing shadows cast by the treetops create a wonderful wilderness feeling on this hike. The frequent pools and small swamps will use up a roll of film (or fill your digital camera).

When the loop rejoins the original trail you probably won't have run into another hiker, and you'll have the opportunity to give some of the things you might have missed a second look. After you stop to look at the wagon wheel again, head over toward the restrooms to find the trailhead for the River Trail, an interpretive hike discussed next in this book.

32

PALMETTO STATE PARK RIVER TRAIL

KEY AT-A-GLANCE INFORMATION

LENGTH: 0.6 miles

CONFIGURATION: Balloon

DIFFICULTY: Easy

SCENERY: Old hardwoods and San Marcos River

EXPOSURE: Mostly shady

TRAFFIC: Light

TRAIL SURFACE: Dirt

HIKING TIME: 30 minutes

ACCESS: Open to day use 8 a.m.– 10 p.m.; $3 entrance fee; Texas Conservation Passport holders are exempt from fees

MAPS: Park maps are available at park headquarters for free

FACILITIES: Indoor toilets with showers, picnic tables, and playground

SPECIAL COMMENTS: Snakes may be present at certain times of year; watch for posted warning signs

IN BRIEF

This short, interpretive trail follows along the bluffs of the San Marcos River, offering good views of the water and local wildlife, including turtles, hawks, and deer. A thick forest of hardwoods is also enjoyed as the path winds through the forest.

DESCRIPTION

This interpretive trail is designed for the nature lover, especially those interested in the plant life of Texas. A guide booklet available at the trailhead corresponds with numbered markers found along the trail. These guides are provided free of charge, but the park asks that you return them to the box when you are done.

As soon as you start down the trail, you'll reach a wood-framed dirt staircase and a sign that reads BUILT BY TROOP 1288. (It is unclear whether the staircase or the entire trail was built by the credited Scout troop.) Follow the stairs to reach the bluff and a good view of the San Marcos River. Be particularly watchful along this section. A lot of brush makes good habitat for rattlesnakes. Numerous holes alongside the trail hint at their presence, so stay on the lookout.

The spring-fed San Marcos River originates 63 miles northwest in the town of San

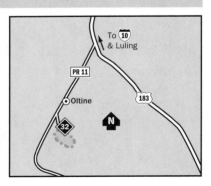

Directions ➔

From Luling, go east on US 183 onto Park Road 11. Park headquarters is about 2 miles down the road. After stopping for your map and to pay entrance fees, continue on the park road and take the second left after the office. Follow the road to a fork and turn left. This is the day-use parking area. After leaving the car, walk toward the restrooms, veering left toward the trail marked "River Trail."

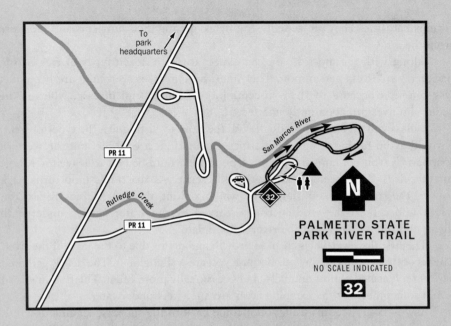

To park headquarters

PR 11

San Marcos River

Rutledge Creek

PR 11

32

N

PALMETTO STATE PARK RIVER TRAIL

NO SCALE INDICATED

32

Marcos. This section is one of the last stretches before it joins with the Guadalupe River a few miles south, near Gonzales. As you walk along the bluffs, you'll notice that the river in this part of the state is very muddy due to the eroding banks that border it. This area is subject to serious flooding, evidenced by the numerous dead logs, brush piles, and flotsam high above the river itself. In spite of the dirty waters, it does make for a good viewing point.

If you've already walked the Palmetto State Park Trail, you'll notice the obvious absence of palmettos in this part of the park. The tree growth here is thick and old. Tall oaks, elms, and persimmons tower over the trail, and the green of leaves is absent at eye level.

The hike follows the edge of the bluff for the first 200 yards before forking right, into the woods and away from the river. Stay to the right. Keep an eye on the tree line for hawks nesting and hunting here.

Along with the hawks' nests, you'll also notice clumps of two types of moss: Spanish moss and ball moss. Spanish moss is more common in the Southeastern United States but also does well here in eastern Texas. The other moss, as its name implies, grows in clumps up to a foot in diameter and is common in the southwestern to south-central regions of Texas. It is often seen growing on non-living surfaces but seems to be doing well here. Despite their appearance, neither form is parasitic. They are actually epiphytes, getting their nutrients and moisture from the air.

Along with the mosses, you can expect to see a dozen types of trees, from hackberry to Texas persimmon. The American elm trees seen here are becoming less common because of their susceptibility to Dutch elm disease, whereas the cedar elm lives on, apparently unaffected.

Unless you are familiar enough with the flora to distinguish the types of trees, I would avoid tasting any of their fruits. Persimmons are edible, but the western soapberry's fruit contains the poison saponin. It would be best to leave the forage for the birds. They seem to know the difference. As the trail's loop turns back toward the trailhead, you'll again be walking along the San Marcos River. You might notice both the eroding banks, carved by the water cutting underneath them, and the two levels of the river's floodplain.

The first (lower) level is clean of growth and debris due to the flow of the river. The second level is more obvious because you are walking on it. The debris gathered here is replenished almost annually, and occasionally more often. The flooding is so severe sometimes that the camping areas are a few feet underwater.

As you complete this trail, you'll come back to the staircase leading down to the trailhead. As long as you're here, take a walk on the Palmetto State Park Trail (see hike 31, page 109).

RED TRAIL AT BASTROP STATE PARK

IN BRIEF

This hike loops through the heart of Bastrop State Park. Begin at a vista overlooking the loblolly pine woods that led to this park's creation, and travel along Copperas Creek through a deep, shady forest reminiscent of east Texas. The moist, intimate stream valleys are also home to the rare Houston toad.

DESCRIPTION

Bastrop State Park is one of Texas's older state parks. It was dedicated in 1937. Land acquisition had been going on for a few years earlier, during the Great Depression. Civilian Conservation Corps (CCC) workers developed the park. The natural reason for its being are the Lost Pines, an isolated pocket of loblolly pines that is mixed with understory species such as oak and yaupon and is separated from similar woods of east Texas by more than 100 miles. At the park's inception, founders didn't realize they were also protecting the greatest concentration of the rare Houston toad, which lives in only a few counties in Texas. The Houston toad is 2 to 3.5 inches long and varies from light brown to gray or purplish gray, sometimes with green patches. They like deep, sandy soils because they are poor burrowers, but they must burrow into the sand for protection from

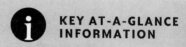

KEY AT-A-GLANCE INFORMATION

LENGTH: 3.3 miles
CONFIGURATION: Loop
DIFFICULTY: Moderate
SCENERY: Deep pine woods, creek valley, oak forest
EXPOSURE: Mostly shady
TRAFFIC: Moderate
TRAIL SURFACE: Pine needles
HIKING TIME: 2 hours
ACCESS: $4/person park-entrance fee
MAPS: At park office
FACILITIES: Restrooms, picnic areas

Directions

From the Austin airport, head east on TX 71 for 25 miles to TX 95 in Bastrop. Turn right and drive north on TX 95 for 0.4 miles to TX 21. Turn right and head east on TX 21 to reach the park, on your right. Pass the park entrance station, then turn left on Park Road 1A and follow it for 1.2 miles to the trailhead, on the right. Start the hike on the Red Trail, near the stone shade shelter.

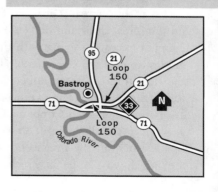

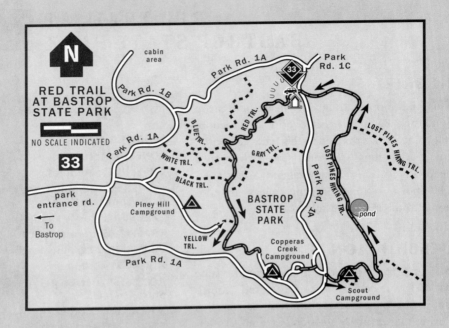

cold weather in the winter and hot, dry conditions in the summer. Pine–oak wood-lands such as those found here are ideal for the toad. For breeding they require still or slow-moving waters, such as Copperas Creek, which is along this trail. Houston toads are active year-round under suitable temperature and moisture conditions. Their diet consists mainly of insects and other invertebrates. The Houston toad population exceeds 2,000 in Bastrop County alone.

This hike through Bastrop State Park starts at the interesting shade shelter, erected by CCC workers on the edge of the Copperas Creek Valley. This round, gazebo-like stone structure beckons you to look inside. Descend from the gazebo by switchbacks on the Red Trail into the valley. Avoid short-cutting the switch-backs, as this increases erosion. Enter rich pine woodland, with red needles fallen on the forest floor and onto the understory oaks and brush. Roll up and down a couple of draws, staying with the red blazes as they moderate the steep hillside grades to meet the Green Trail. This is the first of many trail junctions. Stay with the Red Trail to bridge upper Copperas Creek. Shortly intersect the Blue Trail. Relish the pines soaring overhead and shading the path. Reach the White Trail in a clearing, then span Copperas Creek on bridge with hand rails. Ahead, the Red Trail meets the Black Trail. Shortly, the Grey Trail leads left.

Despite all the intersections, the Red Trail has traveled only 1 mile. Keep moving down Copperas Creek, looking right for the brick remains of an old, defunct water fountain. Rock-hop Copperas Creek before intersecting the Yellow Trail on a small but pretty bluff overlooking Copperas Creek. Soon, open into the walk-in tent campsites of the Copperas Creek Campground. Reach the pavement and walk through the main Copperas Creek Campground, looking for campsite #54. Turn left on the paved road here and take the trail splitting campsites #55 and #56 in a mini-loop. Pay attention here as the trail leaves the mini-loop and comes to a gravel parking area. Veer right here to reach and follow Park Road 1A around a curve.

Ahead at mile 1.7, on the left, is the Lost Pines Hiking Trail and a signboard about Houston toads. Take the Lost Pines Hiking Trail as it passes a side trail leading to a Boy Scout camping area. A water fountain is at the group camping area if you are thirsty. The trail resumes and enters sandy, open ground. Oaks and cedars are more prevalent here. At mile 2.3, turn left at a trail junction, staying away from the main loop of the Lost Pines Hiking Trail. The path descends into a pine thicket, where pine cones, pine logs, and ever-present pine needles are returning to earth. More pines reflect in dark, pine-stained waters of a dammed trailside pond. Beyond the pond, a few small clearings harbor cacti before coming to yet another junction. A sign indicates the scenic overlook, your starting point, as almost 0.5 miles distant. Pass through one last swath of rich, dark woods before climbing to reach Park Road 1A and the end of the loop.

NEARBY ACTIVITIES

The park has two good campgrounds, cabins, and picnic areas and is near the historic town of Bastrop. A 13-mile scenic drive connects Bastrop State Park with Buescher State Park to the east. For more information, call (800) 792-1112 or visit **www.tpwd.state.tx.us/spdest/findadest/parks/bastrop.**

WEST OF AUSTIN

34

FOUR-MILE LOOP TRAIL AT PEDERNALES FALLS STATE PARK

KEY AT-A-GLANCE INFORMATION

LENGTH: 4.8 miles

CONFIGURATION: Balloon

DIFFICULTY: Moderate–difficult

SCENERY: River, wooded plateau

EXPOSURE: Mostly sunny

TRAFFIC: Moderate

TRAIL SURFACE: Dirt, rocks

HIKING TIME: 3 hours

ACCESS: $5/person park-entrance fee

MAPS: Available at park office or online at www.tpwd.state.tx.us/spdest/findadest/parks/pedernales_falls

FACILITIES: Water at trailhead, restrooms at campground

IN BRIEF

This hike circles around a plateau that is bordered on three sides by the Pedernales River, which you must ford to reach the loop portion of the hike. Once on the plateau, you'll earn views of the surrounding Hill Country. This trail is somewhat difficult to follow as many old ranch roads spur from the main path.

DESCRIPTION

This balloon hike has an invigorating beginning. Set off on the River Trail and descend to reach the Pedernales River. Here, you must ford the river, which can be quite chilly in winter. Climb away from the river and circle around a high plateau on an old agglomeration of ranch roads that can be challenging to follow. However, you are rewarded with good views of the Pedernales Valley below and the Hill Country through which it courses. Also, check out the old homesteader cemetery, with simple stone graves.

Leave the Pedernales Falls State Park campground on the River Trail. Pass the campground amphitheater before dropping sharply to the Pedernales River. White blazes painted on trees, stumps, and rocks mark the trail. Get used to looking for these white blazes—they

Directions

This state park is off US 290 at the Hays–Blanco county line, just west of Henly. It can be accessed from Austin via US 290 and from San Antonio via US 281 to US 290. Once at the county line, take Texas Ranch Road 3232 north for 6.2 miles to the park entrance. From the park entrance station, keep going forward 0.7 miles and turn right into the park campground. The hike starts at the River Trail between campsites #33 and #34.

PEDERNALES FALLS STATE PARK

281

34

TX Ranch Rd. 2766

TX Ranch Rd. 3232

To Austin

290

Henly

FOUR-MILE LOOP
AT PEDERNALES
FALLS
STATE PARK

NO SCALE INDICATED

34

4-MILE LOOP

LOOP
SHORTCUT

Pedernales River

PEDERNALES
FALLS
STATE PARK

34

(Parking is
between
campsites
#34 and #33.)

34 33

Pedernales River

trammel
crossing

Regal Creek

primitive
trailhead

park
entrance
station

To Austin
& San Antonio

will help you get around on the far side of the river. For now, the path is easy to follow as it bisects a clearing and then enters a hillside of live oaks. Their limbs form a tunnel through which the trail passes. The Pedernales River comes into view. The green-blue water is appealing to the eye. Cypress trees line the normally clear water. The ford, known as Trammel Crossing, is concrete most of the way across. A long gravel bar and beach lies across the river downstream. Another beach is upstream of the crossing. In the warmer months, folks will be playing in the water here.

Pick up the wide gravel path as it climbs away from the Pedernales on the Four-Mile Loop. The gravel gives way once the trail levels off on the plateau. Small meadows and cacti break up the oak and juniper woodlands. The 5,200-acre Pedernales Falls State Park tract was acquired by the state in 1970. At just over 0.5 miles, reach the loop portion of the hike. Stay right here and keep sight of those white blazes in addition to the scenery. You may also notice old stone arrows on the ground. Go against those arrows. Also, folks have built cairns (stacks of rock) at trail junctions or where old ranch roads spur off. The trail is level now and becomes rocky in places.

The character of the path changes minute to minute. One trail section will pass through a live oak dome; the next section will be grassy with sporadic

The path as it tunnels through live oak

juniper. Reach a junction at 1.7 miles. The outer loop portion of the path keeps forward, heading just east of due north, and the loop shortcut leaves to the left. Keep forward on a slight uphill through open juniper lands, passing an old stone fence at 2 miles that obviously once cut through the open land. Stay on the trail to reach a wire fence and the park boundary at 2.3 miles. Turn left here, tracing the fence line. Begin to look left for a short path leading into the woods and the homesteader cemetery. Here, some graves are in a thicket of juniper and live oak. Old wire fences surround some of the sites, while others have piles of rock marking their location. The names of those interred have been lost to time.

The Four-Mile Loop now makes its biggest climb on the fence line, as views open into the ranch country on its far side. Reach a high point and begin to curve west along the fence line. Tremendous views open to the south as the path descends from the high point. Ahead is a wet-weather drainage, heavily wooded with live oak, juniper, and understory brush that can only be described as lush. The trail climbs out of the drainage to level off in a cactus and grass flat at nearly 3 miles. Turn left here, staying with the southbound white blazes.

The level path makes for easy hiking, and at 3.3 miles you'll reach the intersection with the loop shortcut. Stay right here, still on mostly level trailway, drifting in and out of woodland. Complete the loop portion of the hike at 4 miles. Here, backtrack almost 0.5 miles to the river, making the Trammel Crossing one more time. Ascend away from the beautiful Pedernales to complete your hike.

HAMILTON POOL TRAIL

IN BRIEF

This wonderful hike through a unique geological area is more reminiscent of a walk through a canyon in Colorado than the Texas Hill Country.

DESCRIPTION

Like many of the parks and preserves around the Austin area, Hamilton Pool Preserve has a diverse history. Prior to the 19th century, native Tonkawa and Lipan Apaches lived in this area, though cultural remains have been found that date back thousands of years earlier.

The preserve is named after Morgan Hamilton, brother to the tenth governor of Texas, Andrew Hamilton. Morgan acquired the property in the 1860s, then sold the land in the 1880s to an immigrant German family named Reimer, who wanted it to graze sheep and cattle. It is rumored that the Reimer's son rediscovered a collapsed grotto, and sometime after that the family opened the area for recreational use. For almost a century the area was subjected to unrestricted use, both by frolickers and livestock, and the land suffered greatly as a result. Five years after the Texas Parks and Wildlife Department declared Hamilton Pool the "most significant natural area in rural Travis County," the county purchased 232 acres from the Reimer family in 1985 and implemented plans to restore it to its original state.

Directions

From Interstate 35, take TX 71 west to Hamilton Pool Road/FM 3238. From Bee Cave on TX 71, drive 13 miles on FM 3238 to the preserve.

KEY AT-A-GLANCE INFORMATION

LENGTH: 1.7 miles

CONFIGURATION: Out-and-back with spur

DIFFICULTY: Easy

SCENERY: Ferns, ash junipers, and hardwoods along the Hamilton Creek and Pedernales River; pool and collapsed limestone grotto

EXPOSURE: Shady

TRAFFIC: Light on trail, busy but limited at pool. Weekends are much busier than weekdays.

TRAIL SURFACE: Dirt, rock, and roots

HIKING TIME: 1 hour

ACCESS: Day use only. Open 9 a.m.– 6 p.m.; $5 per vehicle, $2 per pedestrian or bicycle

MAPS: Hamilton Pool Preserve Trail Map is available at the park.

FACILITIES: Composting toilets

SPECIAL COMMENTS: Entrance is limited to 30 vehicles at a time, and once that limit is reached, no one else is let in until some leaves. Plan to arrive early, because there are no places anywhere nearby to wait for cars to leave. Pets are not allowed, and camping and fishing are also prohibited.

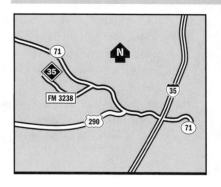

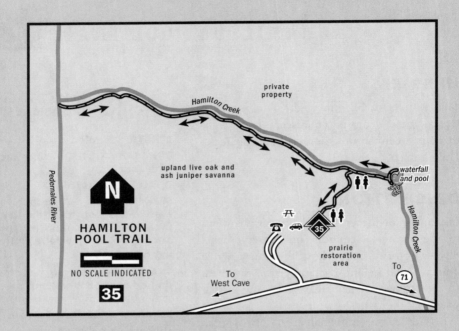

Formed by centuries of water erosion, the canyon provides a natural shelter to a vast array of birds and wildlife. The rich plant life found here is unusual for this area of Texas. Ferns and ash junipers add an almost prehistoric feel to the valley, compounded by the constantly running water of Hamilton Creek. When visiting the park, please help preserve this unique environment and stay on the trails.

The trail starts where the parking lot ends, leading down into the canyon created by Hamilton Creek. A bulletin board at the trailhead displays pictures of the wildlife and plants found inside the preserve. Numerous bird species and reptiles (including the poisonous Texas coral snake) live here. The coral snake is reclusive and usually spends its time hidden in dead logs, waiting for prey. The preserve is also one of the few places in this part of the state where beavers and porcupines are found. Quiet, early morning hikers stand the best chance of sighting these creatures.

About 400 feet into the hike is a bench where you can sit and watch the traffic as it comes and goes to the pool, the most popular attraction of the preserve. The trail is steep at times, and it can be interesting to watch people carrying their ice chests to and from the area. Continue down the trail until you reach a T-junction in the path, where you'll find two portable toilets, garbage and recycling bins, and a directional sign. The pool is on a spur trail to the right, less than 0.1 mile distant, but you'll want to save that until last, so turn left toward the Pedernales River.

The trail parallels Hamilton Creek, which creates a soothing sound as you hike. Many of the trees here are relatively young, though some older trees and the remnants of others can be seen in the form of fallen trunks, logs, and stumps. You'll come to an old dead stump 0.2 miles into the trail, on your right, where you'll see a new tree growing right up through it. Many of the hardwoods here are mesquite, cedar, and oak.

Immediately ahead on the trail, two large boulders lean on each other to form an arch over the trail that taller hikers will have to duck under. Take a moment to study the surface of the rocks, and you'll notice shells embedded in them. Heed a sign here that reminds hikers to remain on the trail to avoid damaging the fragile ecosystem.

Occasional spur trails along the hike include a fork 0.3 miles into the trail that leads down to the creek. At most points, stakes and twine mark the boundaries within which hikers should stay. Where there aren't any such markers, stay on the trail. Gradually the trail climbs, but never too steeply, and eventually winds up about 20 to 30 feet above the creek. As it continues toward the Pedernales, cliff faces become larger along the left side of the trail. Ferns drape the rocks in numerous places, and caves perforate their surface.

At nearly 0.5 miles into the trail, a stand of junipers creates a natural tunnel of foliage. Keep a sharp eye out for birds crossing the path. They could be golden-cheeked warblers, which are known to nest in the park. At just over 0.5 miles, a roped-off scenic overlook affords a view down into the canyon. The water is incredibly clear, due in large part to the numerous small rapids in the stream, and the prospect of seeing fish and snapping turtles (and the occasional beaver) is good. Continue on to the junction of the Pedernales and Hamilton Creek, 0.8 miles from the trailhead.

Once at the Pedernales, two benches made from cedar posts let hikers rest and enjoy the view. The river is very wide here, and the view is breathtaking. When the river is low, numerous sandbars appear; you can wade out and work your toes in the silt and sand of the river. Numerous fish can be seen, and some of them are quite large. These are gar, and they are quite abundant in this stretch of the Pedernales, all the way down to Pedernales Falls State Park. Keep an eye out for great blue herons and egrets wading along the banks. If you brought a snack, this a good place to enjoy it. When you're ready, turn around and start back down the trail.

When you reach the intersection leading back to the parking lot, continue straight to the pool. The sounds of people playing in the waters ahead will precede your arrival. You'll pass between two large boulders just past the toilets, and at 1.5 miles into the hike, you'll see the clear waters of Hamilton Pool, partially shaded by the large outcropping of the collapsed limestone grotto. A small bridge over the creek leads to the pool, but continue up into the grotto itself for now.

The trail leads up into the large, open cave and hugs the inside wall. Almost as soon as you are under its ceiling, a large piece of rock appears, requiring a tight squeeze through the area it's in. A large metal staircase leads down about 20 feet and overlooks the pool. Watch your step, because the stairs are always very slippery.

The small birds you see flying around in the cave are cliff swallows. They make their nests out of mud and hang them like cliff dwellings on the rock wall.

Just as you're exiting the grotto–cave, note a large deposit of lime on the right. Covered in moss, this formation adds the exclamation point to the prehistoric feel of this place. When you're back on the beach, take your shoes off and go for a swim. The water is surprisingly transparent, and fish that get trapped in the pool when the creek is low can be seen circling the banks, looking for a way out. To return to the parking lot, simply cross the bridge, turn right back on the main trail, and head back to the intersection. Climb back up the left fork to find your car.

INKS LAKE STATE PARK TRAIL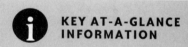

IN BRIEF

Located in the Highland Lakes chain west of Austin, this moderately challenging hike passes through granite hills and wraps around portions of Inks Lake's shoreline. Abundant wildlife and few hikers make this a real gem.

DESCRIPTION

Inks Lake State Park is in the process of improving this trail with a matching grant, and signs of improvements can be found from the beginning. A large sign designates the trailhead and includes a map of the trails available. This hike is composed of a combination of two of them. The third trail leads to the park's primitive camping area and is similar in flora and fauna to this hike.

About 0.2 miles into the hike, after you've walked up a slight rise, look directly out in front of you. On a hill in the distance, you'll notice a local anachronism: a castle sitting atop one of the neighboring hills. Although this is actually a resort and hotel, it certainly is a striking landmark of central Texas. This is definitely another reason to bring binoculars on this hike.

The trails are color coded and are marked accordingly along the trail. The beginning trail's color is green. Following the green markers, begin walking south. The trail starts out wide and easy, with the shade beginning immediately. While you're hiking, you'll encounter slight inclines along the trail, but only a couple of them are steep.

KEY AT-A-GLANCE INFORMATION

LENGTH: 3.6 miles
CONFIGURATION: Balloon
DIFFICULTY: Moderate
EXPOSURE: Shady, with a few open spaces
TRAFFIC: Light
TRAIL SURFACE: Dirt and rock
HIKING TIME: 2 hours
ACCESS: $5
MAPS: Trail maps available from park office
FACILITIES: Restrooms, showers, picnic tables, and camping. Park store sells refreshments and supplies and rents canoes.

Directions

From US 281 (coming from Marble Falls), turn left on Park Road 4, and follow it until you reach the entrance to Inks Lake State Park.

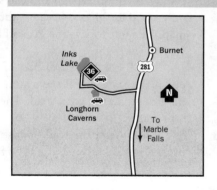

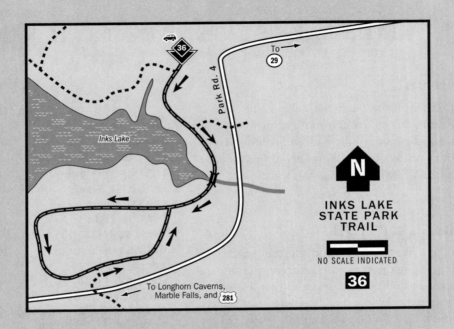

However, the main reason to bring field glasses remains the wildlife. The nature of the foliage along the trail is ideal for attracting fauna. Whitetail deer bed down underneath cedar and oak trees right next to the trail, and an early morning hiker has a good chance of catching the deer while they are still sleeping. Cottontail rabbits are frequently encountered as well.

Near the same point where the castle is visible, the trail forks to the right. The right fork climbs a limestone hill and then leads back to the improved campsites or dead-ends on the lakefront. Stay to the left to remain on the main trail, which follows the lake farther down the path.

The trail continues through the trees and forks again 0.3 miles from the trailhead. Another sign indicates your current location on the trail. Don't rely only on these maps, because they are a little harder to decipher than the park map. The left fork is the Pecan Flats Trail; it leads to the primitive campgrounds. Stay to the right.

You'll climb a small bed of limestone shortly past the fork. A little farther down the trail, you'll see a stone structure through the trees. This is the base of the bridge on the park road. There is also a small wooden bridge on the trail for foot traffic.

From here, the trail opens up, and the lake appears on the right. This area of the lake is know as Stumpy Hollow and is popular with the bass boats as well as bank anglers. Anglers of all ages try their luck for everything from catfish to crawfish.

While hiking along this part of the trail, the odds of spotting wading birds such as blue heron and snowy egret are excellent. Between the months of November and March, there is even a chance of spotting a bald eagle—they nest farther up the Colorado River during the winter.

As you continue to hike, the trail leaves the lake and heads up a hill on more limestone. The peak of this hill, at 962 feet, is actually lower than the trailhead, which is 992 feet above sea level. Keep a keen eye peeled for the trail markers, since no dirt or footprints are here to follow. The markings are green dots of paint rather than arrows. Watch the ground ahead to see more than one marker at a time.

Just before the peak, the trail is again marked with a sign. Although there is no map here, arrows point the way. The right leads through more stone hill, and there is plenty more to the left about 0.75 miles ahead. Take the left fork.

When you reach the next fork, take the left one again. The trail to the right loops back on itself around the hill and heads back to the park, offering little more variety. The left trail crosses the park road and leads back into some thicker land. Shortly after crossing the road, the trail forks again. This time go to the right.

Although there are no benches along this hike, there are plenty of large rocks to rest on. A large group of such rocks is located just past the fork. As you continue on the trail, the markers turn blue and are mainly plastic surveyor's tape in the trees. The trail remains fairly obvious and isn't hard to follow. This section is another loop that circles over two small hills.

One of the most obvious landmarks here is a large power line that you'll pass under twice. When you pass under it the second time, you're about two-thirds through this loop. As you start heading back toward the road, you'll come across yet another fork. The trail to the right is marked in red and is an alternate route to the Pecan Flats campground. Stay to the left and complete the loop back to the park road. Cross the road and follow the trail back to the parking lot, retracing your steps back through Stumpy Hollow.

If you have some time, you might want to head over to the park store and rent a kayak or canoe and explore the coves of Inks Lake. On Thursdays, guides offer canoe tours of the Devil's Water Hole.

37   JOHNSON SETTLEMENT TRAIL

KEY AT-A-GLANCE INFORMATION

LENGTH: 1 mile

CONFIGURATION: Loop

DIFFICULTY: Easy

SCENERY: Historic buildings and longhorn cattle

EXPOSURE: Sunny

TRAFFIC: Moderate–heavy

TRAIL SURFACE: Dirt

HIKING TIME: 20 minutes to walk the trail, but allow more time to explore the settlement

ACCESS: Open year-round, 9 a.m.– sunset

MAPS: NPS map available at visitor center

FACILITIES: Restrooms at the visitor center; dining and shopping in Johnson City

SPECIAL COMMENTS: This area is only part of the Lyndon Johnson National Historical Park. The Ranch, located 14 miles west of town, offers a nature trail (included in this book) and a guided bus tour of the president's home.

IN BRIEF

This is an easy trail that offers a great look at the people who worked the frontiers of the Texas Hill Country, complete with exhibits and artifacts.

DESCRIPTION

The seeds of Johnson City were planted in the 1850s when President Lyndon B. Johnson's grandfather, Sam Ealy Johnson Sr., settled with his brother Tom in a one-room cabin on 320 acres of prime Texas land. The cabin and additional structures eventually became the headquarters for their cattle-driving business, which started a year after the Civil War ended. The brothers drove their cattle north to market from Hill Country, where the demand and the prices for beef were high.

Business was initially very good, so they bought an additional 640 acres to expand their operation. Nestled between the Pedernales and Blanco Rivers, their location was ideal for grazing. The cattle market eventually collapsed, and the brothers ended their partnership in 1871. They left Blanco County, selling their interest in the land to Sam's nephew, James Polk (J. P.) Johnson, after whom Johnson City is named. Many buildings J. P. constructed still exist, including a barn and a cooler house to go with the original cabin. The trail begins across the street from the visitor center. Signs here ask that visitors refrain

----

Directions

From Austin, take US 290 West to US 281 North, and from San Antonio, start on US 281 North. When you reach Johnson City, just follow the signs to the downtown area that point out the park.

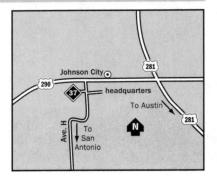

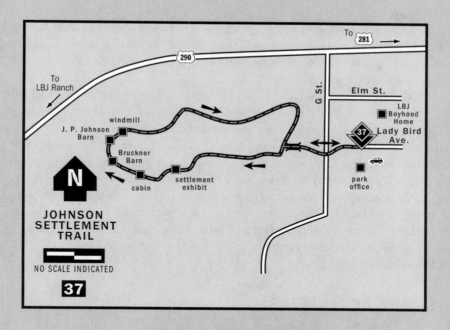

from smoking along the trail and remind them not to climb into the corrals with the temperamental longhorns. The path is wide and easy to traverse, and parents with strollers should have little problem rolling along the packed dirt trail. After crossing a wooden bridge, the trail meanders along the edge of an open field where wildflowers bloom in the spring and early summer. A few old live oaks stand along the trail as well.

You'll reach the interpretive center, which resembles an old ranch house, 0.3 miles from the trailhead. There are numerous rocking chairs on the porch and a huge oak tree in front. The ample shade of this area encourages visitors to sit down, relax for a while, and try to imagine life in a simpler time. There is a breezeway between the restrooms and water fountain.

The self-guided tour inside the center is wheelchair accessible and includes information and artifacts from the early days of the frontier pioneers. One of the highlights of the museum is an actual dialogue composed of correspondence by J. P. Johnson and his fiancée, which has been recorded and plays back for visitors to hear. You can spend an easy hour in here taking in the exhibits.

Past the interpretive center (actually, as you walk through the breezeway), a second bridge leads into the actual settlement area. To the left of the trail is the cedar-fenced corral that contains the longhorns, and another sign cautioning visitors to stay on this side of it. On the right, there is an old covered wagon.

The trail continues toward the original cabin built by Sam and Tom Johnson. The addition of the east room does little to add to the small quarters. The rustic cabin has stood for about 150 years and offers a glimpse into a lifestyle that has long since been forgotten.

A German immigrant named John Bruckner purchased part of the ranch after the brothers ended their business relationship. He is responsible for building the next structure. The cut-stone barn was constructed in 1884. J. P. built the next barn in 1875, along with a two-story frame house that burned down in 1918.

The final structures are a windmill and water tank, and a cooling house built by J. P.'s son-in-law N. T. Stubbs. After having taken enough time to investigate the settlement, you can follow the trail around through the grassland, stopping at a bench located under another oak to watch the birds and animals in the field late in the afternoon. The trail joins a fence and turns to the right. Follow this trail back to the beginning of the loop, where you'll turn left to return to the visitor center.

NEARBY ACTIVITIES

Located across the street from the visitor center is LBJ's childhood home. The former president lived here from age 5 throughout his childhood, until he married at age 26. The home has been restored to its 1920s state and is open for tours to the public.

LYNDON B. JOHNSON RANCH TRAIL

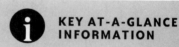

IN BRIEF

A great family hike has historical overtones, wildlife, and interpretive signs. Plenty of rest areas, water fountains, and wide trails make this an easy trip for hikers of all ages. Highlights include a working farm frozen in the 19th century.

DESCRIPTION

The peace and serenity of the Lyndon B. Johnson State and National Historical Ranch offer a stark contrast to the tumultuous time in which he served as president. His ranch house located just on the other side of the Pedernales River was the location of many a lawn chair Cabinet meeting when the tribulations of the presidency would follow him to the quiet of his home. Often referred to as the Texas White House, LBJ succeeded in setting up shop where he was comfortable working, and his staff would fly in to his private airstrip to catch up to him.

This park, along with the ranch that is accessible only by a bus tour, was donated to the nation by LBJ and his wife, a gift to the people and land they were so fond of. The ranch house contains many of the gifts they received while in office.

The trail begins in a large field of wildflowers by the visitor center. The wide path meanders to the northwest toward a stand of

KEY AT-A-GLANCE INFORMATION

LENGTH: 1.1 mile

CONFIGURATION: Balloon with out-and-back spur

DIFFICULTY: Easy

SCENERY: Wildlife pens, working farm, and hardwoods

EXPOSURE: Mostly shady

TRAFFIC: Busy on weekends, lighter during the week and in the mornings

TRAIL SURFACE: Packed dirt

HIKING TIME: 45 minutes

ACCESS: Open to day use

MAPS: Trail map available from park office or online at www.tpwd .state.tx.us/spdest/findadest/ parks/lyndon_b_johnson

FACILITIES: Restrooms, gift shop, and vending machines

Directions

Take US 290 West out of Austin to junction with US 281 North. Take US 281 North to Johnson City and turn left on US 281 West. Park is located 14 miles west of Johnson City on the right. Park in main parking lot and obtain map from park office. Trail begins on the north side of the visitor center and is clearly marked with a large sign.

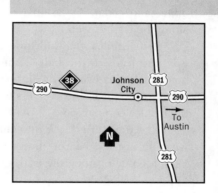

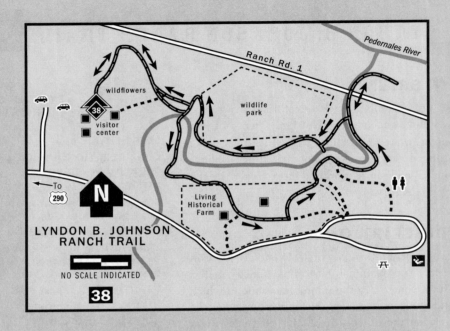

trees. Located 0.1 mile into the hike is a slightly larger-than-life statue of Johnson, who was born and raised in nearby Johnson City. His actual ranch, which has been turned into a national historic park, is just on the other side of the Pedernales River.

As the path continues you'll reach a fork about 0.2 miles into the trail. Stay to the right. You'll see the wildlife pens down the fork to the left. Resist the urge to go look at the deer now, as you'll finish the hike returning along this fork.

Just past the fork, you'll cross a wooden bridge over a nameless perennial stream. The trees are dense here and provide ample shade on a warm afternoon. Signs denote some of the different trees along the path, including hackberry, mesquite, and cedar. Occasional plaques provide information about local wildlife along the trail as well.

At 0.3 miles, the trail forks again. Stay to the right, which loops out a little way and leads to the Hill Country Woody Plant Exhibit and Rest Area. A billboard contains even more information on the local flora and provides a good place to rest weary little hikers who may have to take more steps to keep up with their older companions.

The trail turns back into the main trail after the rest area and leads to the working historical farm almost 0.5 miles into the hike. This is the first of two main highlights along the trail. Open the gate and step back more than 100 years into the past. Forever frozen in the late 19th century, the farmers here go about their daily chores in period costumes and are more than happy to pose for photos. Chickens, turkeys, and other animals wander around the farmyard, and roosters crow for attention all morning long. A large barn and farmhouse make up the structures here, and visitors are free to examine them more closely at their leisure. Just like the period it preserves, there is no rush around here.

Once you've checked out the farm, return to the trail, where it once again forks. The fork to the right leads to a playground area and picnic tables. Unless you plan on taking a break, continue to the left. You'll go through another gate, back into the perennial creek bottom area and the accompanying hardwoods. You'll reach another fork with a bridge to the left. Take the right fork to head to the Pedernales River overlook, passing up another fork to the right, unless you need to use the restrooms at the end of this spur.

Along the trail on the left, which follows the creek bed, you'll find an information plaque on one of the least-heralded animals in Texas: the nutria. A relative of the beaver, this large rodent can be seen on most of the state's rivers and golf course water hazards. They are responsible for most of the holes you'll find dug along trails in the hill country.

Just over 0.5 miles into the hike, you'll walk under a bridge for the ranch road, and more water will be evident in the creek bed, which feeds the Pedernales. The overlook is 0.7 miles into the trail. Here you'll find a great view of what, at times, is a wide and strong river. This is the end of the spur and has another plaque with information on the river's bird and fish life.

After you've walked back under the road, look for a fork to the right. There is a small stone stair that crosses the creek bed. This path rejoins the main trail just on the other side of the bridge you passed up on the way to the overlook.

You'll begin to see the fence of the wildlife pens on the right, and small spurs in the trail allow you to walk up to the high fence for a closer look. On the other side you'll find longhorn cattle and whitetail deer. The cattle are usually lying in the tall grass in the heat of the day, but the behemoths are easy to spot. The deer can generally be seen poking their heads around the trees for a look at the hikers.

When the trail turns to the right, you'll see a water tank on the far end of the pen. Deer are also found here most of the time, and some will even approach the fence, looking for a handout from the passersby. Caution is advised with the friendly deer, because they are still wild animals and can spook easily.

Turn to the left at the next fork, and then right at the next one. One final fork to the left will take you back to the visitor center. Here you can go inside and sign up for the bus tour to the actual Johnson Ranch on the other side of the river; here, the former president and his wife are buried in the family's private cemetery, beneath the live oaks.

39   LONGHORN CAVERN NATURE TRAIL

KEY AT-A-GLANCE INFORMATION

LENGTH: 1.2 miles

CONFIGURATION: Balloon

DIFFICULTY: Easy–moderate

SCENERY: Cedar, oaks, and granite outcroppings

EXPOSURE: Open to shady

TRAFFIC: Moderate

TRAIL SURFACE: Gravel and dirt

HIKING TIME: 45 minutes

ACCESS: Open to day use from dawn to dusk

MAPS: Trail map is available at the park office, but isn't very accurate, or it is available online at www .longhorncaverns.com/backbone map.html

FACILITIES: Restrooms, picnic areas, gift shop, and concession area are open the same hours as the park. Camping, and more hiking, is available at nearby Inks Lake State Park.

IN BRIEF

Just 50 miles west of Austin, the Longhorn Cavern State Park, a 650-acre state park, offers a look at trees and wildlife typically found in the Highland Lakes area. The hike joins the park's two trails as it wanders through cedar stands and passes by and over limestone rocks.

DESCRIPTION

There is a lot of history to Longhorn Cavern State Park. The caverns, after which the park is named, have seen some colorful characters in their time. Apparently, in the 1800s outlaws used it as a hideout. The infamous Sam Bass, who met his end north of Austin in Round Rock, is rumored to have hidden stolen gold here, and local lore suggests that Native Americans held settlers captive here until they were rescued by the Texas Rangers. The nearly 650-acre tract of land was acquired by the state in 1932, and opened as a state park in 1938. Visit the interpretive center to learn more about the cave and the land through which this hike passes.

This is probably one of the easiest trailheads you'll ever have to find. The trail starts right outside the back door of the park office. A sign that reads NATURE TRAIL clearly marks the beginning of the path.

Like many state park trails, the first part of this hike has numbered points of interest that match an interpretive flyer available from the park office. The flyers, however, are

----

Directions

From US 281, north of Marble Falls, take a left on Park Road 4. Longhorn Caverns State Park is on the left.

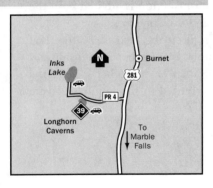

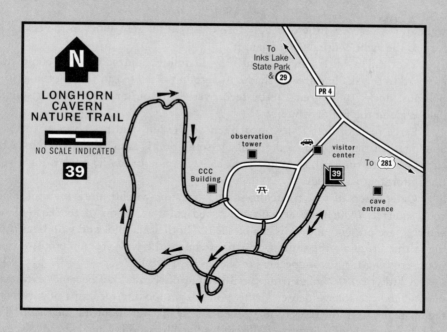

limited in number and may not be available, so you may want to check it out online before you go (visit **www.longhorncaverns.com**). Some of the sites pointed out include types of trees and other flora as well as an outcropping of limestone used as a den by various animals.

This part of the trail is very easy to traverse—ideal for a family hike with kids—and would even allow for a rugged stroller. The path is made of pressed gravel and is wide enough to walk two or more abreast in most places. Although some shade is provided, it is clear enough in some places to warrant a hat and sunscreen.

After walking for a quarter mile, you'll encounter a fork in the trail, where you'll see a garbage can and a bench. A sign points to more hiking on the left. If you're not up for things to get a little more rugged, take the right fork, which will lead to the park road and back to the office. If you wish to continue hiking, take the left fork.

The trail stays the same for a while longer and includes a couple more numbered points, but it quickly narrows to allow for only one hiker at a time. The surface turns to dirt, which can morph into mud if it has been raining. Shortly up the trail you'll encounter yet another fork. Stay to the left to start the loop portion of this hike. Eventually you'll return to this point along the right fork to complete the extended loop.

Another quarter mile up the trail is yet another fork, with a sign reading 3 MINUTE LOOP pointing to the left. This little loop takes less than three minutes to walk and offers very little to see that isn't also on the remainder of the trail. The fork to the right continues the main trail.

The trail is fairly obvious and easy to follow, and at times is completely exposed to the sky and free of shade. At certain times of year, flocks of migrating pelicans, ducks, and egrets can be seen overhead; you may even spot a solitary bald eagle in the fall or winter.

Large beds of limestone can be seen on the left, and prickly pear cactus is abundant on this section of the trail. At some points along the hike, the cactus sticks out into the trail, so watch your step. A spine in the leg makes for a very uncomfortable walk back.

Quiet hikers may be treated to some interesting wildlife along the trail. Black rock squirrels (which are actually a masked color variation of the Eastern fox squirrel) are present, and signs can be seen of both armadillos and wild hogs rooting in the dirt along the trails. Birds that frequent the park are numerous, including everything from woodpeckers to the orchard oriole.

A little over 0.2 miles from the 3 Minute Loop, the trail becomes extremely narrow and the foliage dense. At this point begin looking for strips of surveyor's tape hanging from the trees to mark the trail. Again, watch out for the cactus. The trail surface remains unimproved dirt and is lined by wildflowers and cedar trees.

At numerous points from here on, the trail turns to rock and is impossible to follow without the marking tape. It would be easy to get turned around on this section of the hike. Be sure to scan all directions for the markers when the trail isn't obvious.

As the trail turns south, you'll wind up on a huge bed of limestone surrounded by cedar and oaks. The trail turns a sharp left here. Look for the tape in the trees, but bear in mind that it might not still be there. This is the largest section of rock you'll have been on so far, so you'll know that you should be turning to the left.

Once past the rock, pick up the trail as it begins to widen again as you head for the park road. At the end of this trail there is an old stone building on the left that was built in the 1930s by the Civilian Conservation Corps for use as an office. It's worth a picture. Take the park road to the right from this point to return to the connecting trail.

You'll find the connecting trail less than a quarter of a mile down the road. It is unmarked, but the path is obvious. This will reconnect you to the original trail. Turn left to continue along the previously encountered section, and you will find your way back to the park office. The snack bar will be open, and the iced tea will be cold. If you have time, sign up for the guided tour of the caverns.

NEARBY ACTIVITIES

The park offers guided tours of the caverns themselves regularly. Don't pass up a tour of the unique Longhorn Cavern. Also located nearby is the Canyon of the Eagles Nature Lodge, which offers the Vanishing Texas River Cruise up the Colorado River.

THE LOOP AT ENCHANTED ROCK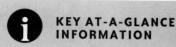

IN BRIEF

Enchanted Rock, arguably the most notable landmark in the central part of the state, is the centerpiece of this loop hike, which encircles the pink-granite mountains that arise from the Texas Hill Country. The breathtaking view from the top of Enchanted Rock extends 360 degrees. Other features along this hike include more vistas, a pond, a canyon, and backcountry campsites. Be prepared to visit during off times, as nice weekends can be so crowded that park entry is cut off.

DESCRIPTION

We'll admit it—Enchanted Rock State Park is outside the distance parameters of this guidebook, but the scenery here is just too good to pass up. Step for step, this is one of the most scenic hikes in central Texas.

Start on the Loop Trail, traveling through open terrain, where views of the surrounding pink granite mountains and boulder fields are far reaching and amazing. You will pass a side trail to a vista before reaching a backcountry campsite. You'll enjoy a water feature, Moss Lake, which makes an excellent front stage for

KEY AT-A-GLANCE INFORMATION

LENGTH: 4.1 miles

CONFIGURATION: Loop

DIFFICULTY: Moderate–difficult

SCENERY: Open-faced granite mountain, broken woods, canyon walls

EXPOSURE: Almost all sunny

TRAFFIC: Very heavy on weekends

TRAIL SURFACE: Granite slab, pea gravel, dirt, rocks

HIKING TIME: 2.75 hours

ACCESS: $5/person park-entrance fee

MAPS: Available at park office

FACILITIES: Restrooms and water at state-park picnic area and campground

Directions

From the Gillespie County Courthouse in downtown Fredericksburg, take Main Street west for 0.3 miles to reach Milam Street, Texas Ranch Road 965. Turn right on Milam Street, RR 965, and follow it for 17 miles, to reach Enchanted Rock State Park. Keep forward beyond the park entrance station, crossing Sandy Creek. Turn left at the T-intersection and park toward campground sites #4–#34. The hike starts on the Loop Trail, at the far side of an auto turnaround, near campsite #22.

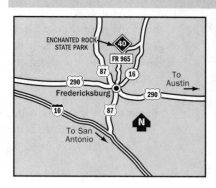

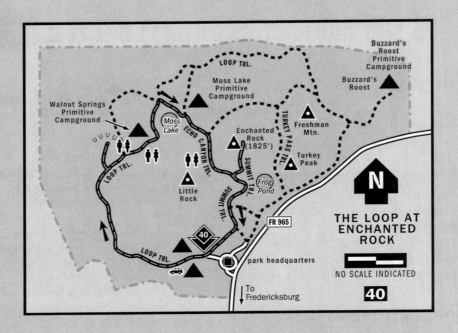

the sheer granite monoliths behind it. Next, travel up Echo Canyon, where the twin towers of Little Rock and Enchanted Rock squeeze the trail. Finally, ascend the open granite face of Enchanted Rock, where vistas open up in all directions.

The rewards are big, but so are the crowds. If you are coming to Enchanted Rock on a weekend, be aware that the park often fills its 260-car capacity by 10 a.m. After this time, automobiles will not be allowed into the park until 4 or 5 p.m., if at all, so plan ahead. You might want to call before you come. The park number is (915) 247-3903. We suggest overnighting at the campground on the weekend of your visit. The campground reservation number is (512) 389-8900. Better yet, come during the week. Avoid this park completely on holidays and during spring break.

Start the hike on the Loop Trail by passing around a metal gate onto a wide pea-gravel path. The terrain is wide open, broken only by smaller tree stands. A boulder field is in the distance. Spur trails head toward any and all rock formations. Rock climbing is popular here. The domes of Little Rock and Enchanted Rock stand to your right.

Begin to walk among cabin-sized boulders, which are strewn about as if they were building blocks tossed by a child. The huge granite slabs beneath your feet will simply amaze you. At slightly more than 0.5 miles, look for a side trail that leads right to an odd standing rock with a hole eroded clear through it—a keyhole of sorts.

Keep in open country, circling around Little Rock, which is little only in comparison to the larger Enchanted Rock. Reach a side trail at 1 mile leading left to a 360-degree vista. You can see other rock formations to the north toward Llano, among other sights.

Ahead, a trail leads left to Walnut Springs Camping Area. This site is for backpackers, but it does have a restroom. Many red oaks are scattered over the landscape. Leave the Loop Trail at 1.5 miles, and then turn right onto the Echo Canyon Trail, soon passing over the dam of Moss Lake. Live oaks offer a shady lakeside resting spot for hikers. The lake and mountains make for a picturesque setting. You can see the sheer granite domes and the boulders that have fallen from the domes over time; in addition, you may see specks of humanity climbing various bluffs and rocks of the domes.

Keep going, heading toward Enchanted Rock, now on a less obvious trail over granite swales. A path leads left for Moss Lake Primitive Camping Area, another backcountry campsite.

Keep straight in this confusing area, aiming for the gap between Enchanted Rock and Little Rock, as an unnamed trail leads left around the north side of Enchanted Rock. You will enter Echo Canyon near a primitive bathroom, and then reach a signboard showing climbing routes and other information. Keep going up Echo Canyon, directly up the rocky drainage amid huge fallen boulders. After passing over a high point, you'll then dip onto a sheer granite slab at 3 miles, at a sign that indicates the Echo Canyon Trail. You can see others scaling the open face of nothing but rock.

Begin angling directly up Enchanted Rock on the Summit Trail. Stay on the hard ground and avoid the few and unusual weather islands, where vegetation struggles for life as a bit of soil has found a home in a crack or indentation in the hard rock. On hot summer days, the sun heats the granite so much that it groans as it cools down after expanding from the heat.

Reach the top of Enchanted Rock, and have a look around. Other visitors will be relaxing and taking in the views, which are plentiful and which expand in every direction. The actual highest point is on the rock's northwest side. Look down onto Moss Lake and the main park area below—you'll see what resembles a world of toy cars, buildings, and people. The landscape of central Texas stretches off for miles in all directions.

Backtrack on the Summit Trail, descending all the way to a feeder branch of Sandy Creek before taking a few steps past a viewing telescope near a gazebo. You are at the far end of the day-use parking area. Follow the paved road toward the southwest end of the campground and complete your loop.

NEARBY ACTIVITIES

This state park offers hiking, picnicking, rock climbing, and walk-in tent camping. For more information, call (800) 792-1112 or visit **www.tpwd.state.tx.us/spdest/ findadest/parks/enchanted_rock.**

LOWER BARTON GREENBELT 41

IN BRIEF

This out-and-back hike travels up the canyon of Barton Creek from Barton Springs Pool at Zilker Park to the MoPac Bridge near Twin Falls. Along the way, you will see rock bluffs overlooking a clear blue stream bordered by riparian hardwood forests as well as drier woods of cedar. The crystalline stream not only has scenic shoals but also deep pools for swimming and stone bluffs popular with rock climbers.

DESCRIPTION

This is, in my humble opinion, one of the best urban hikes in America. The Barton Creek Greenbelt is an oasis of nature in the middle of central Austin. While you're here, you can enjoy a clear stream that has cut a canyon over time, showing off its geologic history in the sheer walls that accompany the stream most of the way. Nature has provided rich vegetation to accompany the rocks and stream, in the form of streamside trees such as sycamore and

KEY AT-A-GLANCE INFORMATION

LENGTH: 8.5 miles
CONFIGURATION: Out-and-back
DIFFICULTY: Difficult
SCENERY: River canyon, riparian woods, clear stream
EXPOSURE: Mostly shady
TRAFFIC: Heavy
TRAIL SURFACE: Dirt, rocks
HIKING TIME: 5.5 hours
ACCESS: Free
MAPS: Online at www.ci.austin.tx .us/parks/greenbelts.htm
FACILITIES: Restrooms, water at trailhead; restroom also along trail

----

Directions ⟶

From I-35 in downtown Austin, take Exit 233, Town Lake/Riverside Drive. Cross Town Lake to reach Riverside Drive. Head west on Riverside Drive and follow it 1.1 mile to Barton Springs Road. Turn left on Barton Springs Road and follow it 1.3 miles to Zilker Park. Turn left again on Barton Springs Road (a park road) and follow it to end in a parking lot just past the Barton Springs Pool entrance. The Barton Creek Greenbelt starts at the west end of the parking area. The safest parking is directly in front of the pool entrance area. Be aware that this trail sometimes closes after rainy periods. If you are in doubt, call ahead; (512) 472-1267.

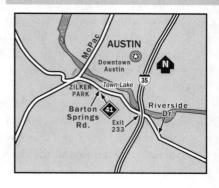

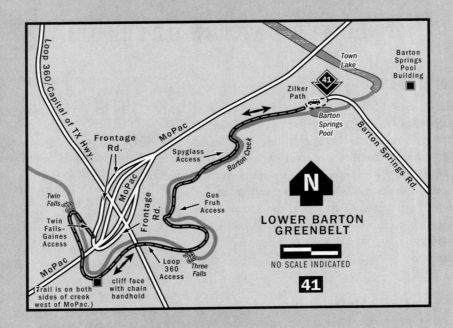

elm. In other places live oak and cedar grow. The entire picture adds up to a wilderness feel, about as wild as you are going to get with skyscrapers and interstates nearby. You will hear the sounds of civilization in the distance, but in other places, you'll hear nothing but flowing water cascading over rocks, continuing to carve and shape this preserve.

Leave the trailhead and begin heading upstream on a gravel path. Barton Creek is to your left as you pass through a field. Shortly enter the canyon of the stream. The trail is marked in quarter-mile increments. The forest-banked creek, which is littered with whitish boulders, forms riffles and shoals. Gravel bars border much of the clear watercourse, where you can easily view the bottom. Bluffs appear at 0.5 miles. Don't be surprised if you see rock climbers plying the bluffs, helmets on, colorful ropes attached.

In places, the trail splits. One route will be for bikers, the other for hikers. In other places, the main trail splits out from previous hikers taking multiple routes. However, it is hard to get truly lost, because the river and the canyon keep you in line.

At 1 mile, the Spyglass Access Trail leaves to the right. A little store sells food and drinks at the road access. A bathroom is near the junction. Beyond here, the canyon widens out and the sky opens overhead. Straddle the divide between the riparian vegetation and the thicker forest.

At 1.5 miles, the trail crosses Barton Creek. Depending on the flow, the crossing may be a wet-footed ford. A secondary path stays upstream without crossing, staying along the edge of a bluff. Rock climbers are frequently over there. The primary path borders lower canyon walls. Look left for a fissure in the wall, forming a small cave. The now-narrow path dips and rolls between trees and over rocks.

At 2.5 miles, the Gus Fruh Access cuts off to the left. A nice gravel bar and contemplation bench overlook Barton Creek here. This is also the point where the Greenbelt crosses over to the right-hand bank as you head upstream. This crossing can be dry over rocks most of the year. Look for deeper swimming holes nearby. Keep upstream in rich woods before the trail returns creekside near a white-walled canyon. More deep pools are here. Reach the Three Falls. Just like it sounds, three back-to-back cascades descend the canyon.

The main trail crosses over to the far bank of Barton Creek just past Three Falls. Again, a secondary trail stays along the right bank, eliminating the ford. The main trail, on the left bank, traverses a boardwalk spanning a side stream. Here, as in many places, separate hiking and biking trails diverge. The hiking trail generally stays closer to Barton Creek. Just ahead, at 3.5 miles, is the 360 Loop Access. A rock climbers' bluff is just across the creek from the 360 Loop Access trail. Keep forward to pass under noisy 360 Loop, Capital of Texas Highway.

Beyond the bridge, the trail drifts away from the creek at times. Many live oaks thrive here. The path narrows, returns to the creek, and begins to hug a bluff line to your left. The bluff narrows so much at one point that a chain has been put into the bluff and footholds have been dug to aid hikers and keep them from falling in the creek. Stay along the bluff line amid some of the Greenbelt's best scenery. Overhanging rock, green ferns, and shade make this a desirable spot on a hot day. A deep pool adds to the mix. The valley widens, and the Greenbelt reaches a very deep pool with a rope swing tied to a live oak. This makes for a good stopping spot, though the MoPac Bridge is nearby. The MoPac Bridge can be your official turnaround spot. However, if you want to make it a 4.5-mile one-way hike, you can end at the Twin Falls–Gaines Access. But you must cross Barton Creek to reach the Twin Falls–Gaines Access. The official crossing (no bridge) is upstream about a quarter mile near Twin Falls. Then you backtrack a bit to reach the 0.2-mile ascent to the access parking area. However, you can just cross over at any shallow spot shortly after the MoPac Bridge. Then keep upstream to reach the access trail. To leave a car at this upper access, see the directions for the Sculpture Falls Hike on the Barton Creek Greenbelt.

NEARBY ACTIVITIES

Zilker Metropolitan Park, at the trailhead, offers swimming at Barton Springs, the Zilker Zephyr (a mini-train to ride), a picnic area, and a hillside theater. For more information, call (512) 974-6700 or visit **www.ci.austin.tx.us/zilker.**

SANDY CREEK HIKE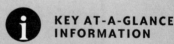

IN BRIEF

This hike at Enchanted Rock State Park is often overlooked by the more popular trek to the top of Enchanted Rock. It is certainly less busy as it travels along clear Sandy Creek, past Frog Pond, then through the pink granite mountains that make the Enchanted Rock area so beautiful. The trail is a little hard to follow in places as it loops back around to Sandy Creek.

DESCRIPTION

This hike avoids the throngs that can be heading up Enchanted Rock yet enjoys much of the same scenery. Cruise along the valley of Sandy Creek, crossing over to reach the Frog Pond. From here, take the Turkey Pass Trail, cutting between Enchanted Rock and Turkey Peak, where granite walls rise on both sides of the trail. Work through a smaller wooded canyon nearing Buzzard's Roost (Buzzard's Roost and Turkey Peak are both rock-scrambling destinations). Return to your destination along the open, pretty Sandy Creek.

The heavy use at Enchanted Rock has resulted in many illegal bootleg trails running

KEY AT-A-GLANCE INFORMATION

LENGTH: 3 miles
CONFIGURATION: Loop
DIFFICULTY: Moderate–difficult
SCENERY: Creekbed, granite mountains
EXPOSURE: Mostly open
TRAFFIC: Moderate to busy
TRAIL SURFACE: Dirt, gravel, rock
HIKING TIME: 2 hours
ACCESS: $6/person park-entrance fee
MAPS: Available at park office
FACILITIES: Restrooms, water at trailhead

Directions

From the Gillespie County Courthouse in downtown Fredericksburg, take Main Street west for 0.3 miles to reach Milam Street/RR 965. Turn right on Milam Street, Texas Ranch Road 965, and follow it for 17 miles, to reach Enchanted Rock State Park. Keep forward beyond the park entrance station, crossing Sandy Creek. Turn right at the T-intersection and park. The hike starts near the gazebo and restrooms. However, do not take the Summit Trail. Instead, head for the low water concrete footbridge crossing Sandy Creek.

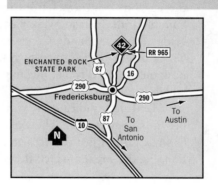

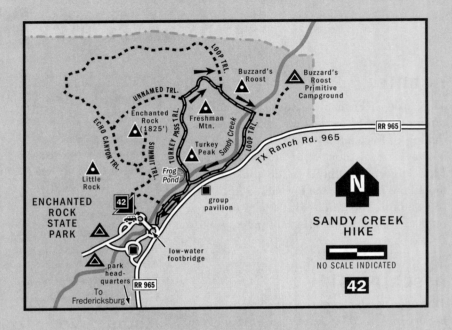

just about everywhere. The legal trails, which are better to follow, are marked with a low wooden posts inscribed with an arrow and a white plastic diamond. Get used to looking for this sign—certain sections of the hike are hard to follow.

If you are coming on a weekend, the park often fills its 260-car capacity by 10 a.m. After this, cars will not be allowed into the park until 4 or 5 p.m., if at all. Plan ahead. You might want to call before you come. The park number is (915) 247-3903. I suggest overnighting at the campground on the weekend of your visit. The campground reservation number is (512) 389-8900. Better yet, come during the week. Avoid this park on holidays and during spring break.

From the northeast end of the day-use parking area, near the restrooms and the gazebo, head away from the throngs heading up Enchanted Rock on the Summit Trail. Instead, walk past the bathrooms for the low-water concrete foot-bridge spanning Sandy Creek and heading toward the park office. Cross Sandy Creek on the bridge, then turn left, passing through a small picnic area. You are now on the right track, heading downstream in the floodplain of Sandy Creek, which is to your left.

Trail signs indicate the way as you shortly travel under a cathedral of shade providing hardwoods. The walking is easy. Reach a group picnic pavilion beside Sandy Creek at just over 0.5 miles. Turn left here on the Turkey Pass Trail, rock-hopping the stream, which flows in clear braids over a grainy, tan bed. Frog Pond

Rock slab between hills near Sandy Creek

appears just over the hill from Sandy Creek. Walk along the pond's edge before reaching a junction. Stay right on the Turkey Pass Trail, heading for the gap between Turkey Peak to the right and Enchanted Rock to the left. This is one place where multiple paths spur off, especially toward Turkey Peak, which hikers often climb. The mammoth stature of Enchanted Rock towers to your left.

Reach the gap and keep forward. The trail travels over slabs of granite, making for a wide-open panorama. Freshman Mountain stands in the distance to your right. Broken pieces of granite, in all shapes and sizes, lie at the base of Enchanted Rock. Gravity is obviously doing its work. Drift down through oak woods to reach a trail junction at just over a mile. The Turkey Pass Trail ends here. Turn right onto an unnamed trail, immediately crossing a wet-weather drainage. Keep downstream, parallel to the drainage, before climbing over a hill and dipping into the drainage again. Look for the trail signs. The trail briefly follows the bottom of the drainage before leaving left to join the Loop Trail at 1.6 miles. Buzzard's Roost, a prominent rock formation popular for climbing and scrambling, is dead ahead.

Turn right on the wider, easier-to-follow Loop Trail. It travels amid boulder fields and other pink granite features between Freshman Mountain to your right and Buzzard's Roost. This area beckons exploration. Descend to cross Sandy Creek. Just ahead, the trail leading to Buzzard's Roost Primitive Camping Area leaves to the left. You, however, continue upstream along open Sandy Creek, where gravel bars and many rock formations enhance the stream shed. Views open of Turkey Peak, then of Enchanted Rock up high.

Return to the group picnic shelter at 2.4 miles. This ends the loop portion of your hike. Keep forward along Sandy Creek and backtrack a little more than 0.5 miles to the trailhead.

NEARBY ACTIVITIES

This state park offers hiking, picnicking, rock climbing, and walk-in tent camping. For more information, call (800) 792-1112 or visit www.tpwd.state.tx.us/spdest/findadest/parks/enchanted_rock.

SCULPTURE FALLS HIKE AT BARTON CREEK

43

IN BRIEF

This out-and-back hike begins midway along the Barton Creek Greenbelt. Leave the busy Twin Falls–Gaines Access and descend into the Barton Creek canyon. Once in the canyon, head upstream, passing Twin Falls before reaching Sculpture Falls. The deep pools by both falls make for alluring swimming holes.

DESCRIPTION

The Barton Creek Greenbelt is one of Austin's outdoor treasures and is enjoyed by an abundance of outdoor enthusiasts, not only to hike but also to rock climb, mountain bike, and swim. This particular section of the Greenbelt has two waterfalls/swimming holes, making it very popular. It may be the busiest stretch of trail in this entire guidebook. So when you come here, try to make it during the week. In the morning would be even better. The often-busy trail leaves the often-busy MoPac Highway, cruising along the rim of the canyon before angling down toward Barton Creek. The first waterfall, Twin Falls, is shortly upstream. Keep forward, traveling beneath tunnel-like woods to reach Sculpture Falls, another wide drop over a rock shelf.

The trailhead has a signboard to help orient you. Pass the signboard and walk a few

KEY AT-A-GLANCE INFORMATION

LENGTH: 3 miles
CONFIGURATION: Out-and-back
DIFFICULTY: Moderate
SCENERY: River canyon, waterfalls, rich woods
EXPOSURE: Mostly shady
TRAFFIC: Very heavy
TRAIL SURFACE: Dirt, rock
HIKING TIME: 2.5 hours
ACCESS: Free
MAPS: Online at www.ci.austin.tx .us/parks/greenbelts.htm
FACILITIES: None

Directions

From MoPac, Loop 1, south of the Colorado River, take the exit for Loop 360 south, Capital of Texas Highway. After getting off MoPac, keep south on the frontage road rather than actually getting on Loop 360 north or south. The Twin Falls/Gaines Access is on the right side of the frontage road before it loops back under MoPac.

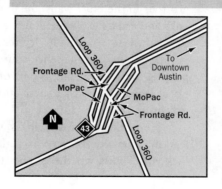

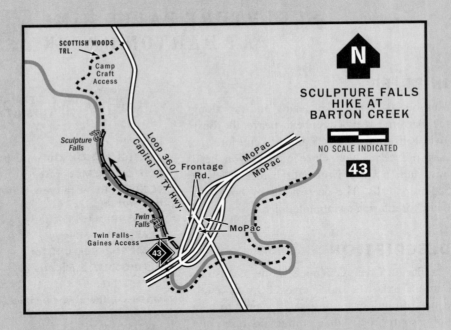

steps to the rim of the canyon. Cedar trees collectively shade the dirt path. Head right, upstream, though Barton Creek is far below. Shortly descend on a graded trail to reach a post at 0.2 miles. The trees are much thicker and taller here in the riverine woodland of the canyon.

Clear-blue Barton Creek flows on your left. Head upstream. You will notice how the heavily used path braids into numerous paths cut by multiple users. Twin Falls is just ahead. Here, the creek gets backed up before collecting energy and then pushing over a rock shelf in two different channels to make deep pools. The pool closest to the trail is very popular with swimmers escaping the heat of a Texas summer.

Keep upstream, passing a gray and tan bluff. Look for eroded overhangs and grottoes in the bluff walls. Small riffles and shoals noisily accompany hikers. Live oaks and cedars grow seemingly everywhere but the trail, forming a tunnel around the path. Pass a normally dry feeder branch coming in from your right. Past this point, look for a stone fence coursing through the woods. This fence runs roughly parallel to the creek and is part of a group of walls, circles, and other formations. Local legend has is that these rock formations were part of a failed Spanish mission from the early 1700s.

Here, the trail really splits apart. Side trails lead down to the creek; others lead into the woods away from the water. Others run side by side up the canyon. Pick your route, whether it goes through the deep woods or along the stream.

The far side canyon walls have grown tall on nearing Sculpture Falls, forcing the alternate trail on that side of the creek to ford at a spring beside Barton Creek. Reach Sculpture Falls at 1.5 miles. Barton Creek descends over a dimpled shelf of rock. A long, deep pool forms below the low, wide drop. The rock shelf continues on the far side of the stream. If you can rock-hop over there, the shelf makes for an excellent relaxing spot for lunch or sunbathing—or simply to toss your shoes off and take a dip.

From Sculpture Falls, the Barton Creek Greenbelt continues 1.3 miles farther, ending with a climb up a steep hill known as the Trail of Life. The hill climbs 300 feet in 0.3 miles, ending at a neighborhood off Scottish Woods Trail. This trailhead is known as the Camp Craft Access. The many "No Parking" signs around the trailhead make leaving a car here a risky endeavor. Your best bet is to make this an out-and-back hike, whether you go to trail's end or not.

NEARBY ACTIVITIES

This section of the Barton Creek Greenbelt offers mountain biking, swimming, and rock climbing. For more information, call (512) 974-6700 or visit **www .ci.austin.tx.us/parks.**

44   WOLF MOUNTAIN TRAIL

KEY AT-A-GLANCE INFORMATION

LENGTH: 7.4 miles
CONFIGURATION: Balloon
DIFFICULTY: Difficult
SCENERY: Mountainside oak–juniper woods, creek valleys
EXPOSURE: Mostly sunny
TRAFFIC: Moderate
TRAIL SURFACE: Dirt, rocks
HIKING TIME: 4.5 hours
ACCESS: $5/person park-entrance fee
MAPS: Available at park office or online at www.tpwd.state.tx.us/spdest/findadest/parks/pedernales_falls
FACILITIES: Water at trailhead, restrooms at park office and near backcountry camping area on trail

IN BRIEF

This trail explores the high country of Pedernales Falls State Park. Good views await, as do creeks, a spring, and even a homesite. This rustic swath of the Hill Country offers a true sense of remoteness. For those inclined, the Wolf Mountain Trail also has a backcountry campsite, which can extend your adventure. A side trip to the Pedernales River adds even more beauty.

DESCRIPTION

This is a solid day hike in the Hill Country. This trail is great to hike after a rain-bearing front has blown through, filling the Pedernales River and its tributaries and clearing the skies for far-reaching views. The path ventures across several stream sheds, the last of which has a spring and homesite nearby. Ascend Wolf Mountain to take in vistas of the land beyond and the Pedernales River below.

The Wolf Mountain Trail descends from the parking area into juniper woods to reach a roadbed used only by park personnel. Veer right here, descending past a feeder branch of Regal Creek. A small cascade falls here in times of flow. Climb away, shortly noticing the signs that mark the path in half-mile increments.

Directions

This state park is off US 290 at the Hays-Blanco county line, just west of Henly. It can be accessed from Austin via US 290 and from San Antonio via US 281 to US 290. Once at the county line, take Texas Ranch Road 3232 north for 6.2 miles to the park entrance. From the park entrance station keep forward 0.2 miles and turn right at the sign for primitive camping and reach the trailhead.

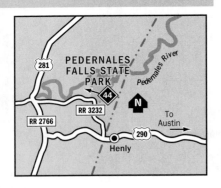

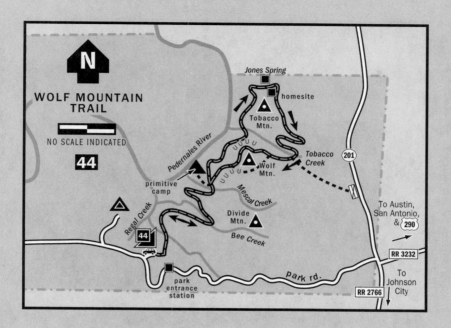

Oak-and-juniper woodland dominates the landscape, which is broken by rough grasses and rocks aplenty. Gray skeletons of long-dead trees litter the landscape. Curve into the Bee Creek watershed, reaching Bee Creek at 1 mile. Ascend away from Bee Creek, passing a high point at 1.5 miles. Wolf Mountain is visible ahead on the downgrade from the high point.

Reach Mescal Creek at 1.8 miles. Climb a bit, then reach a trail junction. Here a path leading left heads toward the primitive backcountry camping area for overnight visitors. This is also a way to access the Pedernales River. The area below the river bluffs is especially scenic; however, no camping is allowed below the bluffs. Day hikers continue forward to reach another junction and the loop portion of the hike. Keep straight here, shortly passing a primitive backcountry privy. The woodland thickens in spots. Dip down to Tobacco Creek at 2.6 miles. This creek dries up earlier than the other creeks. Pass a grassy meadow just after the 3-mile mark. Ahead, at 3.3 miles, is Jones Spring on a side trail to the left. The spring is set in a creek bed. When the stream is flowing, the water falls in a series of cascades. Look for ferns growing on the north bank of this creek bed.

Ahead on the Wolf Mountain Trail are the rock walls of an old homesite. Undoubtedly, the homesteaders decided to build here because of the close proximity

Hill Country near Wolf Mountain

to Jones Spring. The trail narrows to a single-track path beyond the homesite as it twice bisects an old stone fence. While you are walking, contemplate all the hard labor that went into building that fence. Keep ascending along a normally dry streambed amid a thicket of live oaks, deciduous oaks, and junipers.

Turn away from the streambed you have been following just before the 4-mile marker. Ascend a rock slope with a more arid look to it. A real sense of remoteness falls over the land here. The narrow path, ascent, and multitude of rocks make the hiking slower than on the old roadbed. Reach a trail junction at mile 4.6. Veer right here, joining an old roadbed. The trail leading left heads to the park boundary and Blanco CR 201. Shortly ahead is another trail junction. Veer right here, although either way takes you around the peak of Wolf Mountain. The right, or east, side has better vistas. The vistas quickly open up, and you can look out far in the Pedernales Valley and beyond. Ahead, there are points where you can see the unmistakable green-blue color of the river itself. At mile 5.2, meet the trail that came around the west side of the mountain. Descend, looking left for a narrow side trail that leads uphill to a wooden viewing platform.

Reach another junction at mile 5.4. You have been here before. Turn left, backtracking now, passing the backcountry camping area, Mescal Creek, and Bee Creek, returning to the trailhead at 7.4 miles.

NEARBY ACTIVITIES

Pedernales Falls State Park has camping, fishing, mountain biking, river swimming, and tubing. For more information, call (800) 792-1112, or visit **www.tpwd .state.tx.us/spdest/findadest/parks/pedernales_falls.**

SAN ANTONIO

45   COMANCHE LOOKOUT LOOP

KEY AT-A-GLANCE INFORMATION

LENGTH: 1.7 miles
CONFIGURATION: Loop
DIFFICULTY: Moderate
SCENERY: Cedar forest, hilltop vistas
EXPOSURE: Mostly open
TRAFFIC: Moderate–busy on weekends
TRAIL SURFACE: Asphalt, gravel, concrete
HIKING TIME: 1.25 hours
ACCESS: Free
MAPS: None available
FACILITIES: Water fountain near old tower

IN BRIEF

This hike travels up to and around a historic hill northeast of San Antonio in a suburban park. The trail surface varies from asphalt to gravel to concrete as it ascends to an old tower with stupendous views of San Antonio, then circles around the hill.

DESCRIPTION

My, how San Antonio has grown and changed over time! What once was an eclectic residence on the edge of town, and before that a native Indian watch post, has now turned into a suburban park, where residents can enjoy a vista purely for pleasure and get a little exercise in the meantime. The hike leaves the trailhead on busy Nacogdoches Road and follows a paved path up to Comanche Lookout, where you can see the surprisingly tall tower of the former residence. From here, circle down and around a hill to make a surprisingly rewarding and invigorating hike. If the distance is a bit short for your taste, just do the hike all over again, or make your own trek using the myriad gravel paths that wind throughout the park.

The unnamed paved path leaves the trailhead and begins a rise through scattered juniper and mesquite trees. A concrete path soon leaves to the left. This is your return route. Keep following the asphalt trail uphill, passing a second concrete path crossing the asphalt trail. Before

----

Directions ⟶

From Exit 172 on Interstate 35 north of San Antonio, take Loop 1604 west 1.5 miles to FR 2252, Nacogdoches Road. Head west on Nacogdoches toward San Antonio, 1 mile. Trailhead at Comanche Lookout Park will be on your right.

[Map: Loop 1604; Comanche Lookout Park; 45; To Austin; 35; Exit 172; Loop 1604; To Downtown San Antonio; 35; Nacogdoches Rd; FR 2252; N]

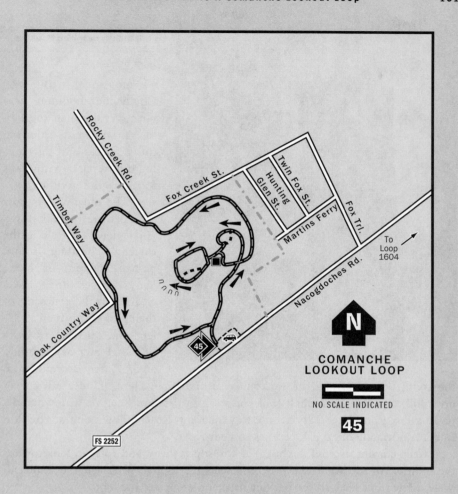

too long the asphalt path makes a turnaround atop the hill. From here, head south and the old tower comes into view.

Comanche Lookout is the fourth highest point in Bexar County, at 1,340 feet. The Apaches, then the Comanches, used the hill as a vantage point for warfare and hunting. It was also a landmark for travelers in the 1700s. The Camino Real leading from San Antonio to Nacogdoches traveled past the hill. Your access road, Nacogdoches Road, traces the old Camino Real.

Comanche Lookout changed hands several times after Texas was settled. In 1923, one Edward H. Coppack bought the land. He was a history buff and envisioned a medieval-style castle atop the hill. His compound included a four-story stone tower. After Coppack died, his children sold the land to a developer who tore down all but the stone tower, which still stands today. In the early 1990s,

Hill Country near Wolf Mountain

a movement to save Comanche Lookout was born, resulting in the city of San Antonio acquiring the 92 acres and developing it as a park (with plans for more in the future).

The old tower is now fenced in. However, for a good view, keep along the ridgeline heading south, past the lookout. In places, live oak trees thrive, but a clearing at the south tip of the hilltop affords an excellent and far-reaching vista of the greater San Antonio area. Curve around from the south point, passing the lookout a second time. Here, a side trail curves downhill, crossing the asphalt trail you took to the top. Keep on a downgrade, passing Fox Run Elementary School to your right. Reach a low point at Fox Run Road. A normally dry creek bed lies to your right.

Keep curving around the hill. The forest gives way, and you can look toward the hilltop. All too soon, the path intersects the asphalt trail near the trailhead. Walk a few steps back to the parking area and complete the loop.

NEARBY ACTIVITIES

This park is centered on the Comanche Lookout and is primarily a hiking and walking park. For more information, call (210) 207-8480, or visit **www.sanantonio .gov/sapar.**

FRIEDRICH PARK TRAIL  46

IN BRIEF

This is a rugged hike in a pristine Hill Country preserve with a 350-foot climb, steep and narrow trails, and an abundance of Texas plant life. The Friedrich Wilderness Park is also home to one of the oldest working windmills in Bexar County.

DESCRIPTION

If not for Norma Friedrich Ward, the 232-acre Friedrich Wilderness Park would not be a reality. In 1971, Ms. Ward bequeathed 180 acres of this land to the city of San Antonio in memory of her parents to ensure that the native vegetation and wildlife would be protected. An additional 52 adjacent acres was donated by W. L. Mathews and Associates. Now the Friends of Friedrich Wilderness Park, in conjunction with San Antonio Parks and Recreation, maintains a stewardship role to this unique resource that offers more than 5 miles of trails.

Unlike some local parks, Friedrich Wilderness Park has an extensive trail system open to wheelchairs. Each trail is rated, indicating how appropriate it is for wheelchair use. Levels 1 through 3 are open to wheelchairs and indicate increasing difficulty. Level 1 trails have gentle slopes and are paved with either asphalt or concrete, whereas Level 3 trails consist of crushed-stone surface and slopes are significantly steeper. Wheelchair users are cautioned that exceptional upper-body strength

KEY AT-A-GLANCE INFORMATION

LENGTH: 2.3 miles
CONFIGURATION: Loop
DIFFICULTY: Difficult
SCENERY: Thick hardwoods, limestone, and endangered songbirds
EXPOSURE: Shady
TRAFFIC: Light
TRAIL SURFACE: Concrete, dirt, roots, and rock
HIKING TIME: 1.5 hours
ACCESS: 8 a.m.–5 p.m., October–March; 8 a.m.–8 p.m., April–September
MAPS: Van Raub (USGS); trail map available at park kiosk and online at www.sanaturalareas.org/fp/fptrails.html
FACILITIES: Restrooms
SPECIAL COMMENTS: The Friedrich Wilderness Park is a very delicate ecosystem, and rules require that it be treated as such. No pets are allowed. Fires and smoking are also prohibited. Bicycles are not allowed. For more information, call the Friedrich Wilderness Park at (210) 564-6400.

Directions

Take I-10 West from San Antonio, and then take Exit 554 to Camp Bullis Road. Stay on the access road until you can turn west on Oak. When you reach the end of Oak, turn north—the park is right on the left.

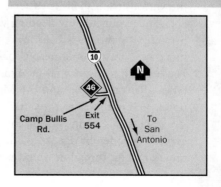

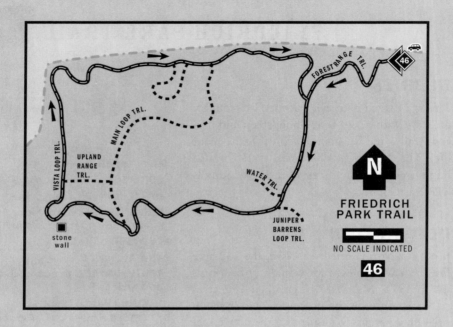

may be required. Level 4 trails are unimproved dirt designed to be difficult to traverse. They may include rock ledges and steep gradients and are not accessible to wheelchairs.

The trailhead at the southwest end of the parking lot provides access to all of the park's trails. You'll see a bulletin board and kiosk with information about the park, as well as a desk with a Plexiglas cover containing trail maps, a bird list, and a guest book for visitors to sign.

A flyer titled "Emilie and Albert Friedrich Wilderness Park" also contains a trail map and interpretive information to correspond with numbered points along the various trails. This is easier to read and carry than the photocopied map.

Start your hike by heading west on the concrete Main Loop Trail. The shade provided by the trees help make this hike a little more bearable on an otherwise hot day. There are numerous benches located at the beginning legs of the trail. You'll reach a T-intersection about 450 feet into the trail. The Forest Range Trail takes off to the right, and the Main Loop, designated as a Level 2 trail from this point on, continues to the left.

The trail changes from concrete to asphalt as it continues up the hill, then across a wooden bridge over a dry creek bed. Several sections of fencing are visible on your right, though it is unclear what purpose they serve. Another T-intersection is reached at 0.3 miles. You will return to this point later using the trail on your right, so head left to continue on the southern portion of the Main Loop Trail. The trail surface turns to mulch as you keep traveling the Main Loop, and the incline starts to increase. Three hundred feet ahead, the trail forks. Continue on the Main Loop Trail, or go right on the more rugged, Level 4 Water Trail, which rejoins the Main Loop. About 0.1 mile past the intersection of the Main Loop and Water Trail, you'll reach the Juniper Barrens Loop Trail, which appears on your left. Continue right along the Main Loop Trail, which becomes a Level 4 trail from this point. The trail surface is dirt and rock from here on out.

As the incline steadily increases you'll see a bench on the left; this is the last place to sit for a while. After you've climbed about 200 feet (to 1,390 feet elevation), a sign informs hikers that the remainder of the park has been set aside as protected habitat for the black-capped vireo. These small songbirds make nests from the bark strips of the ash juniper tree (also called the mountain cedar) found in this area. One of the main reasons for the vireo's decline is habitat loss, though they also fall prey to the parasitic nesting of the brown-headed cowbird. These larger birds lay their eggs in other birds' nests and abandon them to be raised by the nest's owners. The young cowbirds usually hatch first and crowd out the other chicks.

You'll come to another sign with the park's map system on it and find a fork in the trail. The Main Loop continues to the right, but go left on Vista Loop Trail, which rejoins the Main Loop in about a mile. Go up the hill to reach the park's highest point (1,440 feet) 1 mile into the hike. Enjoy the great views of the surrounding area. Nearby you will see a wall constructed of stacked limestone that crosses the trail and disappears north into the brush. The trail leaves the wall behind, becomes very narrow and rocky, and soon loops back to rejoin the wall, turning north to follow the rock wall for several tenths of a mile. Shortly after rejoining the wall, you'll come to an intersection with the Upland Range Trail, which leads 0.1 mile back to the Main Loop Trail. Stay on the Vista Loop Trail.

The trail is now on the backside of the hill you just climbed, and the view to the west is expansive. Miles of hills and valleys roll on with very little sign of civilization. You'll reach another sign about the black-capped vireo habitat and shortly thereafter see a set of earthen stairs leading down. The dirt and root surface of the trail requires that you watch your step. The trail is very narrow at this point, and steep gradients leave no room for error on the left side. Occasionally, wooden planks have been added to shore up the trail against erosion. Another set of earth-and-wood stairs at just over 1.5 miles lead down into and back out of a small canyon.

Shortly after the stairs, you'll reach the Fern Del Trail on your right. If you haven't felt challenged enough, take this short, steep loop trail, which rejoins Vista Loop Trail. Otherwise, continue on, passing the other end of Fern Del Trail 0.1 mile later. You'll soon meet back up with the Main Loop trail and a sign noting you are 0.5 miles from the trailhead. Turn left and go mostly downhill from this point. Having climbed back out of the valley you were in, you'll be able to hear the traffic that was inaudible on the opposite side of the hill.

The hike ends on the same trail it began on, and the downhill slope is a welcome change. The cement trail leads back to the parking lot, past the kiosk you passed on the way in to the park. Sign the guest book if you haven't already, and be sure to note any birds you may have sighted in their log.

HILL VIEW TRAIL

IN BRIEF

Located north of San Antonio, this wild area serves as a retreat for bikers, joggers, and hikers. Pet lovers can also enjoy this hike through natural Hill Country woodland that includes a stop at an observation tower overlooking the city.

DESCRIPTION

This park is just one more of the many wild places located within a stone's throw of the city. Even from the parking lot, the park looks more like a playground than a nature preserve. This may be a benefit to keeping the area as natural as possible. Even so, a surprising number of people seem to be in the know. Even weekday evenings bring out a good number of people looking to get away from the bustle of the workday.

The hike begins in the large group picnic area on the south side of the park. Wherever you wind up parking, you'll be walking south to get to the trailhead. There is usually a birthday party or company picnic going on here, so looking for the crowd can be just as effective. A restroom is located between the lot and the pavilion that serves as party headquarters. Don't let the crowds dissuade you; things will get much quieter soon. In this area there are a couple of billboards with various flyers and a trail map. A letterbox contains paper maps of the trail that you can take along with you.

KEY AT-A-GLANCE INFORMATION

LENGTH: 3.2 miles

CONFIGURATION: Loop with balloon spur

DIFFICULTY: Moderate

SCENERY: Typical Hill Country woodland, abundant wildlife, and dog lovers

EXPOSURE: Mostly shady

TRAFFIC: Moderate

TRAIL SURFACE: Cement, rock, asphalt, and dirt

HIKING TIME: 1.5 hours

ACCESS: Open for day use, 6 a.m.–dark

MAPS: Available at trail entrance

FACILITIES: Picnic tables, restrooms, and campsites available by permit.

SPECIAL COMMENTS: Camp Bullis Training Site, a military reservation, borders the park, so don't cross any fences. Bicyclers use the park, so watch for them as you enter.

Directions

From Exit 558 on I-10 north of San Antonio, take Loop Road 1604 eastbound to Northwest Military Highway. Exit from Loop Road 160 north on Northwest Military Highway and follow it 2 miles north to the trailhead.

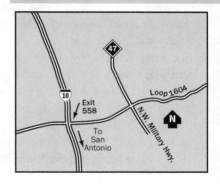

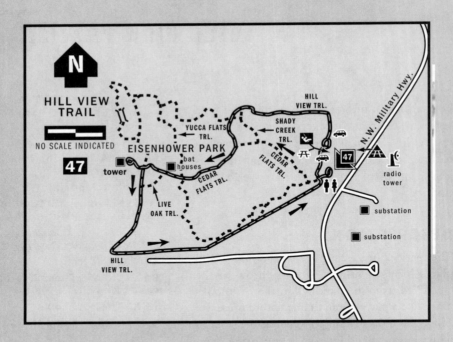

Follow the signs to the Hill View Trail, and walk behind and to the right of the picnic area. The trail at this point is cement and part of a larger trail system. The trail forks 0.2 miles into the hike, where directional signs show the choices before you. To the left lies a rock trail named Hill View N (for natural). The other trail is the Hill View paved trail that continues forward to an exit in the parking lot and back from where you came. Take the trail to the left to get off the beaten path.

The surrounding hillside is typical of the terrain first encountered by settlers arriving in this area of Texas, and it looks deceptively fertile. However, the dense mesquite, hackberry, and cedar as well as the thriving saw grass and yucca hide the rocky soil, which is of little use for farming. The inhospitable soil is what steered the early settlers toward the sheep and cattle industries. With the exception of grazing, there's not much more this land will support.

Keep hiking down the trail until you see a spur that looks more like a game trail than a hiking trail. Ignore this path, which leads to the off-limits military reservation, and continue a little farther until you reach a junction just over 0.5 miles into the hike. This one is legitimate and is clearly marked. The Shady Creek Trail to the left is a short loop off the paved Cedar Flats Trail that will reconnect with this trail farther ahead. Stay on the path you're on for now. Soon the second Shady Creek junction joins the trail. At this point, turn to the left and take the Shady Creek Trail.

This trail joins the paved Cedar Flats trail in about 350 yards. Take the Cedar Flats trail to the right, and start toward the observation tower at the top of the hill.

Located at an intersection of three trails, the observation area sits 1.2 miles into your trek. Here, the natural Yucca Flats Trail (to the right) leads to the permit-only campsites and loops back eventually into the parking area to the left. The Live Oak Trail, also a natural surface, leads straight ahead and up the hill, joining the Hill View loop south of the observation tower. The third trail is the Cedar Flats Trail, and it, too, continues up the hill and takes you to the tower.

On the left side of the trail, partially obscured by a large tree, sit two benches overlooking a clearing on the opposite side of the trail. Look for the white plywood banners, marked with a bat silhouette—nearby shelters help attract bats to the area, but their presence is not as reliable as in other areas of the state.

Just past the benches, the Cedar Flats Trail intersects the Hill View Trail, on which the hike began, at 1.3 miles. Signs mark the trails at the junctions, and a restroom stands on the left side of the paved trail. From this point, the Cedar Flats Trail continues toward a small loop and the observation tower. The Hill View Trail loops back toward the trailhead at both ends. Continue up the paved trail for 0.1 mile to visit the tower. The Holly Hills Optimist Club built this wooden structure in 1984, and it shows minimal wear after so many years. Constructed of 4x4 beams, it resembles the modern play areas found in most parks these days, and a staircase leads up two flights to the observation platform. The view from here is vast, to say the least. At 1,290 feet, this is the high point of the park. The view encompasses the rolling hills to the north and west, as well as San Antonio to the south. Loop 1604 and its traffic are visible 2 miles south of the park. A large quarry operation is also visible from the tower.

After taking a break to enjoy the view, return down the Cedar Flats Trail to the junction with the Hill View Trail. From this point, remaining on the paved trail will take you back downhill to the trailheads and parking lot. The Hill View loop to the right takes a roundabout path to the same destination and offers a chance to view more of the bird and animal life of the park. Follow the natural Hill View Trail to the right.

Depending on the time of the day, the chances of seeing whitetail deer coming out of their hiding places are very good. On most hikes here, I've been able to hike within a few yards of the wary creatures. Cottontail rabbits, roadrunners, and even wild hogs can also be seen among the yucca, mesquite, and prickly pear.

The trail surface switches from rock to dirt and is very easy to traverse at this point in the hike, which meanders downhill for the rest. Joggers and dog walkers just beginning their hikes start to appear from down the trail. At 1.7 miles into the hike, a spur to the left, marked by a sign as the Live Oak Trail, leads into the thick and eventually joins the Cedar Flats Trail.

At 2.2 miles the trail meets with a high fence, which it parallels for the remainder of the hike, and turns left. This begins the last leg of the hike, and the trail is mostly level from this point on. High-current power lines buzz overhead, carrying their load to a transformer station across the street from the park. Three miles into the hike you'll see the park's baseball field on the other side of the fence. A concrete jogging trail is also visible to the left. The trail ends in the pavilion area in which it began, just a few yards from the map sign. Check the bulletin boards for information on upcoming interpretive programs being held be various clubs and groups in the park.

LEON CREEK VISTA
AT O. P. SCHNABEL PARK

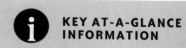

IN BRIEF

This walk makes a loop at one of San Antonio's most visited parks. Often used by walkers, bikers, and dog enthusiasts, this trail curves along the bluffs overlooking Leon Creek, where you can view the city. An additional concrete walkway winds through other parts of the park.

DESCRIPTION

This walking trail is convenient for those living in San Antonio northwest of downtown. O. P. Schnabel Park is well maintained and attractive, offering many other activities in addition to walking. The trail makes a convenient loop amid fine scenery and is topped off with a good view. The convenience and attractiveness draw the crowds, though. On weekend afternoons you may be hard-pressed to find a parking spot. Despite the crowds, the trail has its regulars who walk, jog, or lead their dogs. Try to hit this spot on the off-times and it may become part of your routine. Be aware that mountain bikers will be plying the myriad dirt trails spurring off the paved and concrete loop.

In 1964, the city of San Antonio purchased this property where French Creek runs south, eventually meeting Leon Creek downstream. The many oaks were the initial

KEY AT-A-GLANCE INFORMATION

LENGTH: 1.2 miles
CONFIGURATION: Loop
DIFFICULTY: Easy
SCENERY: Cedar forest, bluff
EXPOSURE: Mostly shady
TRAFFIC: Very heavy
TRAIL SURFACE: Concrete
HIKING TIME: 1 hour
ACCESS: Free
MAPS: None available
FACILITIES: Restrooms, water, play area, pavilion at trailhead

Directions

From the junction of Loop 1604, Anderson Loop, and TX 16 Bandera Road, head south on Bandera Road for 1.7 miles to the O. P. Schnabel Park entrance, on your left. Turn into the park and reach a T intersection. Turn left and you'll shortly reach the Sadie Ray and Waldo Graff Pavilion. The trail starts near the pavilion.

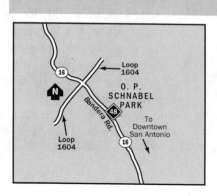

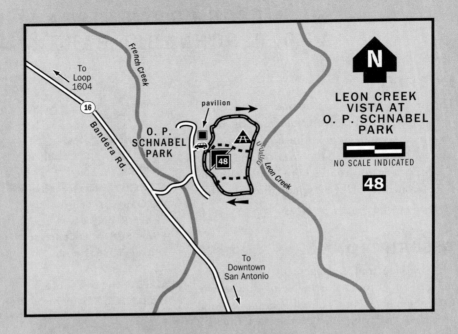

drawing card at what was then called Bandera Road Park. In 1977, the park was renamed after O. P. Schnabel. He had built a reputation in town for his anti-litter campaigns based around such sayings as "nice people don't litter," and "be a beauty bug, not a litter bug." His detractors said his initials stood for "Old Pushbroom." Schnabel's good works live on at the Beautify San Antonio Association, which he helped found. Today, housing developments have sprung up both north and south of the park, leaving the park as a nice little suburban niche of green amid the sprawl. Ball fields, picnic areas, and additional paved trails have been built, attracting even more visitors.

Leave the Sadie Ray and Waldo Graff Pavilion on an asphalt trail. Immediately turn left onto a concrete path. Keep alongside a picnic and play area. A mixture of cedar, oak, and grass line the path. At 0.2 miles, the trail runs into a T-intersection at the park's northern edge. Houses back up to the park fence. Turn right here, climbing slightly. Come around to reach a high point near a transmission tower. Pass alongside the tower. Gain views from the bluffs that you are straddling. At 0.5 miles, reach a tin-roofed pavilion. A concrete side trail leads to a cleared overlook. The valley of Leon Creek lies below. The bulk of San Antonio spreads out to the south and east.

Keep south on the bluff line beyond the overlook. Many dirt spurs dip off the bluff. Curve away from the bluff line as you approach the houses on Tippit Trail. The path begins to curve back toward the parking area. Meander west, then north beneath cedar trees thick enough to provide more-than-adequate shade. Pass a path that shortcuts the main loop. Return to the parking area and complete the loop. You are at the south end of the large parking area near the pavilion.

If you are interested in doing a little more walking, look for the concrete trail leading away from the pavilion back toward Bandera Road. The trail immediately crosses the park road near the pavilion and heads around park facilities to loop across French Creek.

49   McALLISTER PARK TRAIL

KEY AT-A-GLANCE INFORMATION

LENGTH: 3.6 miles
CONFIGURATION: Figure-8
DIFFICULTY: Easy
SCENERY: Thick woodland park with an abundance of wildlife
EXPOSURE: Shady
TRAFFIC: Heavy
TRAIL SURFACE: Asphalt
HIKING TIME: 1.7 hours
ACCESS: 5 a.m. to 11 p.m.
MAPS: None
FACILITIES: Restrooms and water fountains at the main pavilion

IN BRIEF

A lot of things go into making a good hike, and McAllister Park has most of them. Location, accessibility, flora, and fauna combine to make this trail, located right in San Antonio, well worth the trip.

DESCRIPTION

Located on the north side of town near San Antonio International Airport, this 856-acre park is well maintained. Apparently, few people know about its existence, but those who do use it often. Although there is no official trailhead, the path can be accessed from numerous parking areas, allowing you to shorten your hike if you don't have time to walk the whole thing.

To get the most distance out of the trail system here, this hike starts at the southeast corner of the park. There are only a few places where you double back on previously hiked sections. After parking, walk toward the baseball fields until you see the trailhead on your left. This is where you'll start.

The trees grow close to the trail, and there is little room off either side of the path to wander unimpeded. Wide enough to walk two abreast or to allow joggers and bicyclists to pass the slower walkers, the paved trail is well shaded and allows a feeling of solitude for most of the hike.

As you make your way along the trail, you'll reach a T-intersection. The trail to the

- -

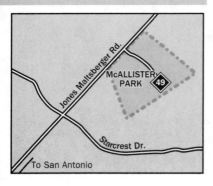

Directions ⟶

From US 281 in San Antonio, turn east on Nakoma Street, which becomes Jones Maltsberger Road. Continue about 1.5 miles, and the park will be on your right.

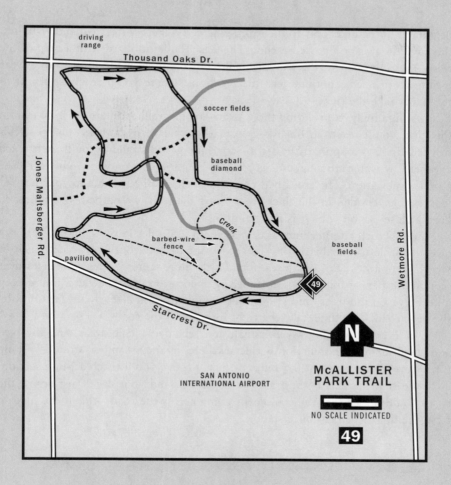

right leads around the baseball fields and rejoins one of the loops. Take the trail to the left. At 0.7 miles into the trek, you'll see the pavilions you passed when you drove into the park. There is a trail intersection and a road crossing here. Continue going straight, unless you need the restrooms located at the pavilions.

You'll find another side trail to your left 0.3 miles from the pavilions, when you reach Jones Maltsberger Road on your left. Stay on the main trail to the right. The trail skirts the edge of the park, and there is a driving range on your left, so keep an eye out for stray balls until you're safely past it. You'll be out of range when you reach the first low-water crossing after the driving range. You'll notice several houses on the left of the trail as you continue, and you'll reach a second low-water crossing. After this crossing the baseball fields are again visible, and there is a side trail to the left. This is the same side trail you passed at the beginning of the hike. Stay to the right, where you'll cross the road and walk into the pavilion area you passed earlier. There is a bulletin board with a map of the trail—the only map of the trail available. Once you've made use of any of the facilities you need, continue past the pavilions, where you'll reach a turnoff to the right. Take the right.

Astoundingly, considering there is no official trailhead here, at 2 miles into the hike, you'll reach an obelisk-style marker that reads 2 MILES. Just past this marker, there is a spur to the right—continue going straight. You'll then reach another low-water crossing, and as you come up the rise, on your right you'll see a police substation. The creek bed you just crossed will be visible to your left but inaccessible. Hidden in the thick trees along the trail is a barbed-wire fence, so keep a close eye on your pets and children.

You'll reach another intersection at about 2.5 miles into the hike. There is a trail to the left, and this is the one you want to take. Both trails lead back to where you parked; this one just offers a little more scenery. The number of deer seen in this park is impressive, considering its location inside the city limits. Keep a keen eye on the trees, and you should see plenty. You'll reach another fork by the park road. This time, take the right fork across the road.

You'll begin skirting several small and secluded picnic areas, and the bird and small mammal population is thickest here, as they scamper around looking for leftovers. After almost 0.5 miles of picnic areas, you'll reach a T-intersection. Take the right, as this is the trail you began on, and your car is just across the road. You'll notice that the trail keeps going across the road—this is the link-up from the fork near the police station.

PANTHER CANYON TRAIL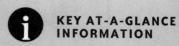

IN BRIEF

This is a surprisingly scenic hike up a lush canyon in Landa Park, a New Braunfels city park that is worth visiting in its own right. In addition to enjoying the scenery, you can enhance your knowledge of the canyon's flora and fauna with interpretive information available at the park office. Deer are often spotted in the depths of the canyon. Give yourself plenty of time to enjoy not only the trail but the rest of Landa Park as well.

DESCRIPTION

The trail begins at Comal Springs, the headwaters of the Comal River, around which Landa Park is centered. However, Panther Canyon is dry, heavy rains excepted. Along the way, you will crisscross the wet-weather streambed beneath rich woodland covering the canyon floor and hills. Sheer rock bluffs add a scenic touch to the walk. Landa Park also has a paved walking and jogging trail that winds through the park. Stop by the park office to pick up the interpretive guide

KEY AT-A-GLANCE INFORMATION

LENGTH: 1.6 miles
CONFIGURATION: Out-and-back
DIFFICULTY: Moderate
SCENERY: Wooded canyon
EXPOSURE: Mostly shady
TRAFFIC: Moderate, busy on warm-weather weekends
TRAIL SURFACE: Rocks, dirt
HIKING TIME: 1 hour
ACCESS: Free
MAPS: At park office or online at www.nbtexas.org/DocumentView.asp?DID=129
FACILITIES: Restrooms, water fountains at park

Directions

From Exit 187 on I-35 in New Braunfels, take Seguin Avenue west, going around the town square. At 1.4 miles, veer left onto Landa Street from Seguin Avenue. Follow Landa Street to enter Landa Park. Turn right into Landa Park and keep forward on Landa Park Drive, crossing the Comal River a total of three times (the first crossing is just after you enter the park). After the third crossing and total of 0.6 miles, look right for the parking area beside a spring wading pool. Comal Springs is just across the street from the parking area. The Panther Canyon Trail begins just beyond the springhead.

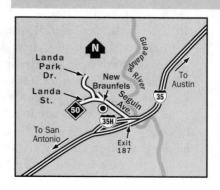

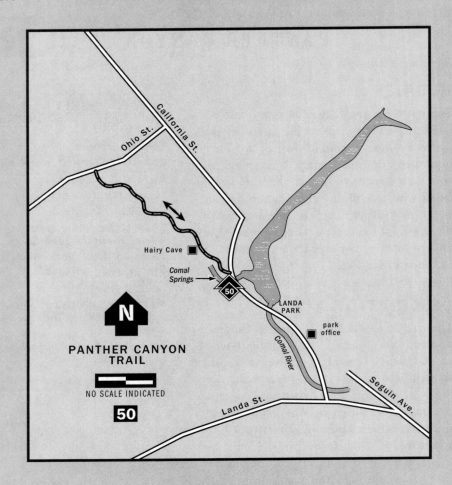

PANTHER CANYON TRAIL

NO SCALE INDICATED

for the Panther Canyon Trail. Numbered posts along the trail correspond with the interpretive literature.

Landa Park and Comal Springs have an interesting history. Located along the Balcones Fault, the springs, heralded as the biggest springs in Texas and the Southwest, issue forth from the Edwards aquifer. The level land of the park area was a popular camping spot for Texas's Native Americans. Many artifacts and burial sites have been found around the springs. A Spanish mission was built here in 1756. Later, German settlers came to the area, naming the community New Braunfels. William H. Merriweather bought the Comal Springs tract in 1847, building a cotton gin and gristmill. Joseph Landa later purchased it. In the late 1800s, the area known as Landa's Pasture became a popular picnicking place.

Checking out Comal Springs

Comal Springs' reputation as a tourist destination grew, attracting a railroad line and hotel. Excursion rails ran from San Antonio and Austin, carrying passengers to visit and bathe in the springs.

The Landa property was sold, and the tract suffered during the Great Depression and was eventually closed as a park. The closure prompted the city of New Braunfels to purchase the property in 1936. Since then, the park has been expanded with additional purchases and development, becoming the destination it is today.

The Panther Canyon area was one of the later purchases forming the modern Landa Park. Stop and check out Comal Springs at the trailhead. The water is clear, cool, and clean as it busts directly out of a limestone wall. The spring harbors the endangered fountain darter, a small fish. Pass the spring and enter the surprisingly narrow, deep, and natural Panther Canyon, which contrasts greatly with the balance of the wide-open, manicured park. Immediately cross the first wash. Overhead is a wealth of trees, including live oak, elm, buckeye, and mountain laurel.

At a bench, look across the canyon for a small cave, really more of a narrow, tunnel-like opening. This is an old spring mouth, now dry. It is known as Hairy Cave. During the summer, the cave is so thick with granddaddy longlegs that the inside appears to be hairy! Try to keep quiet as you ascend the canyon. Deer are present here—you may see one, especially if you're here in the morning and evening.

Keep crisscrossing back and forth over a rocky streambed. Watch for sheer, moss-covered walls. The canyon opens up and widens in places. Here, the hardwoods grow over a pretty grassy understory. The trail curves with the canyon, continuing to ascend. Side washes come in occasionally. At nearly a mile, reach the park boundary near a private residence to your left. This is a good turnaround spot. However, an informal path continues up the canyon to Ohio Street and New Braunfels High School.

NEARBY ACTIVITIES

Landa Park is a fun destination. Here, you can not only hike but also swim in a spring-fed pool or an Olympic-sized conventional pool, picnic, ride a mini-train, and fish. Other pastimes include golf, miniature golf, and tennis. The park also has a concrete walking and jogging trail. The nearby Guadalupe River has tubing in summer. For more information, call (830) 608-2160 or visit **www.nbtexas.org/index.asp?NID=156.**

SAN ANTONIO BOTANICAL GARDENS TRAIL

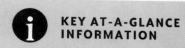

51

IN BRIEF

An educational jaunt located just north of downtown San Antonio attracts people from around town and beyond. The garden offers exhibits of local and exotic plant life that serves the secondary purpose of attracting a wide variety of bird life to the area.

DESCRIPTION

The San Antonio Botanical Garden was opened in 1980 as a living museum to help educate people to the role plants have in the environment. A popular spot for educational outings, this hike is a better way to learn about the local flora than trying to identify plants and trees from books. Three simulated Texas ecological areas highlight the garden, as well as modern-looking, pyramid-shaped greenhouses.

The guest center, the Daniel Sullivan Carriage House, is listed in the National Register of Historic Places. Constructed in 1896, it was moved stone by stone from its original location downtown to its current location. In fact, almost all of the structures were brought from other places and have some historical value. The carriage house now contains the Carriage House Kitchen and the Garden Gate Gift Shop. This is where you pay the entry fee and enter the gardens.

Outside the carriage house the path leads up a set of stairs (a ramp for wheelchairs and

---

Directions

From US 281 in San Antonio, exit on Hildebrand Avenue east. Turn right on New Braunfels Road, then left on Funston. The garden is on the left. For more information, call (210) 207-3250 or go to www.sabot.org.

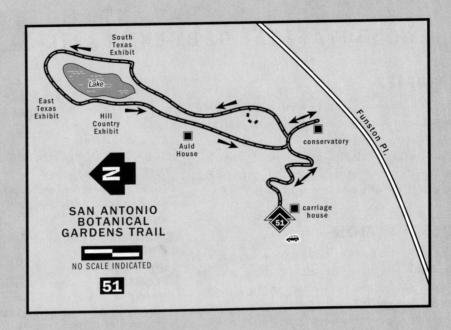

strollers lies beside the stairs). You'll see a plaque at the top of the stairs with a map of the park, the same map shown in the brochure. There is a signpost with arrows pointing every which way. Head to the stairs in front of you to continue the hike. At the top of the stairs you'll see a large natural canopy of vines and a fountain in a courtyard. Turn left on this side of the fountain to visit the Texas habitat areas.

The path forks, and a ramp with handrails leads up a light incline. There is also a dirt path in front of you, which you should follow. Unlike the interpretive hikes in the outlying parks, the botanical garden has signs identifying all the different trees and plants. Shortly after the path are a set of stairs leading down into the conservatory and a path leading around a hill with a gazebo perched on top. At the next two trail junctions, continue going straight. There is a stone wall here and a small aqueduct on the left side of the path. The path forks at nearly 0.5 miles; the flagstone path goes off to the right, and the path you're on continues left and turns to dirt. The one-acre lake before you is indicative of those found in east Texas. A nearby gumball-type vending machine allows visitors to purchase food for the numerous ducks that live by the lake. Where the trail Ts up, take the path right (toward the east-Texas exhibit) to begin the first loop of the hike.

The path that encircles the lake turns to mulch and has a lush canopy that shades the trail. Immediately to the right stands a small palisado-adobe building. This south Texas exhibit area showcases the trees and shrubs found in the southern part of the state, such as mesquite, blackbrush, and ebony. Notice the roofs of the two buildings are made from native plants.

The trail continues under the canopy to the east Texas area. Pines, sweetgums, and magnolias stand out as you look over the lake to the left. The ducks here are more than willing to remind you about the other feed machine near the shore. On the right side of the trail stands a log cabin and accompanying storage shed, both relocated from a 95-acre farm in Park, Texas, that was flooded by a new reservoir. The display even includes a garden with tomato and pepper plants.

When the trail forks again, stay to the left, continuing around the lake. A sign pointing to the Hill Country display reminds you that you're on the right track. The plants here—like mountain cedar and laurel—are native to the Texas Hill Country, and area residents should be familiar with the majority of them. You can also see the Schumacher House. Built in 1849 from wood, mud, and sand, the structure was relocated from Fredericksburg. The next building on the trail, the Auld House, though not original, was based on a cabin in Leakey and is available for rental. There is also a patio, water fountain, and restrooms.

Past the Auld House, there are a couple of garden areas with flagstone sidewalks, and you can see the visitor center to the right and the gazebo to the left on top of its hill. As you stroll through the wildflower trail on the way to the aforementioned garden areas, notice the size of the Hill Country live oak standing on the trail. You'll also see ball moss on the branches of the tree. Continue on to the garden areas, and then turn left back toward the fountain you passed when you came in.

At this point you can return to the carriage house or turn left and go to the Lucille Halsell Conservatory. These modern-looking greenhouses hold exhibits of European plants and flowers and trees from South America and Asia. The climate-controlled greenhouses offer an area to cool off in on a warm afternoon and probably hold any plants you expected to see in other areas of the garden that you didn't find.

52   SAN ANTONIO MISSION TRAIL

KEY AT-A-GLANCE INFORMATION

LENGTH: 6 miles

CONFIGURATION: Out-and-back

DIFFICULTY: Very easy

SCENERY: Historic Spanish missions and the San Antonio River

EXPOSURE: Open

TRAFFIC: Moderate to heavy

TRAIL SURFACE: Asphalt

HIKING TIME: Walking time is about 1.5 hours, but allow extra time to explore the missions

ACCESS: Open for day use

MAPS: Available from the park office at Mission San Jose, or online at www.nps.gov/saan/planyour visit/maps.htm

FACILITIES: Restrooms, gift shop, and picnic areas with barbecue pits

SPECIAL COMMENTS: Though considered historical sites, the missions are still active worship centers. The park service asks that you respect services and parish staff.

IN BRIEF

Stroll between two historic missions along the historic San Antonio Mission Trail. Visit the remains of these cultural centers of the past, and enjoy the surprisingly lush trail that connects them.

DESCRIPTION

The San Antonio Missions National Historic Park consists of a chain of four missions along the San Antonio River—San José, San Juan, Espada, and Concepción. These structures, in conjunction with the Alamo, form the oldest chain of Catholic missions in North America. Originally lured here by rumors of wealth and the encroaching French from Louisiana, the Spaniards established these missions in east Texas hoping to take advantage of the local riches. Failing this, they set about converting the locals to Catholicism.

The first mission built in the area served as a waypoint between the missions in Louisiana–east Texas and New Spain (Mexico). This was the Mission San Antonio de Valero, later known as the Alamo. Two years later, in 1720, Fray Antonio Margil de Jesús established a second mission, San José, for the purpose of converting the native Coahuiltecan tribes. In the meantime, the east-Texas missions failed; three of these missions were relocated to the San Antonio area. The missions soon became

----

Directions ⟶

From Interstate 35, exit at East Southcross Boulevard. Proceed west on Southcross to Roosevelt Avenue. Turn left and proceed south on Roosevelt until it intersects with Napier Avenue. Turn left. The visitor center is on your left.

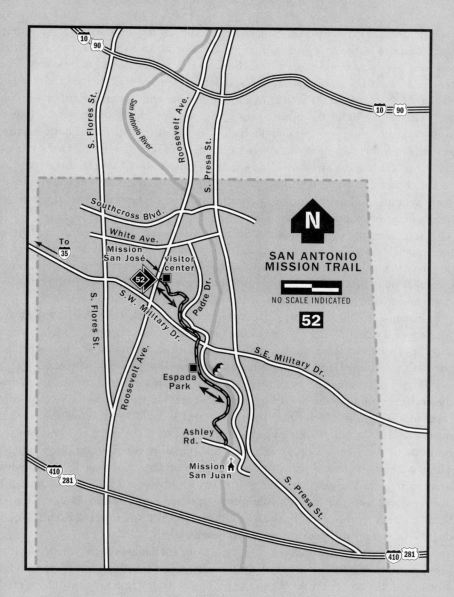

not only religious centers but cultural and economic centers as well, complete with fortified walls, farms with an irrigation system, and herds of sheep and cattle.

Currently, the best trail exists between the Mission San Jose and the Mission San Juan, though the National Park Service plans to complete a trail from the Alamo south to the Mission Espada. The visitor center and park headquarters are located at the Mission San José, where the hike begins.

Before starting your hike, explore the remains of the old mission at a leisurely pace. The size of the San José mission led to its being known as the "queen of the missions"—it was considered an excellent model for other Texas missions. The center of village life and the source of its defense, the large walls helped the resident Native Americans fend off attacks by raiding Apache and Comanche tribes.

The beginning of the hike is very open, and depending on the time of year, you'll want to bring sunscreen and a hat. The asphalt trail surface is quite narrow at first. With the exception of the length, there is no reason why children couldn't enjoy this trail, and a stroller would be easy to push along. The trail starts at the visitor center and heads south across the parking lot area, reaching Padre Drive. Turn right and follow the trail as it parallels the road. The trail passes a fenced-in field where sheep are still kept today.

Soon after the sheep enclosure, the trail widens and you'll arrive at the first of four footbridges; another lies just ahead. The path reaches the San Antonio River at just over 0.5 miles and continues beside it. The trees here are thick enough, however, that most of the time the river is hidden from view. The wide path continues south and reaches a small parking area known as Padre Park at 1.4 miles.

Pass under Military Drive, than arrive at Espada Park 1.8 miles into the trail, where you'll find parking spaces, picnic tables, and grills set up for public use. A short way south of the park, the path separates from the road, which crosses the river at the Espada Dam, and continues along the west bank of the river.

The trail is wide and in very good shape, and it's more pleasant for leaving the traffic behind, albeit briefly. Shortly after leaving the road you'll come to a third footbridge, at which point the trail stands about 40 feet above the river at normal levels. As you walk along this section, look to the right and you can see portions of the Acequia de Espada, the remains of a gravity-flow ditch system. These *acequias* remain as part of a larger system of dams and aqueducts that were used to irrigate the missions' fields for agricultural use. The Espada Dam still diverts water into the Acequia Madre, or "mother ditch," which is carried over Sixmile Creek by the oldest Spanish aqueduct in North America, the Espada Aqueduct. This system still provides water to nearby farms.

Continuing southward, you'll reach a stone embankment on your right that prevents further erosion and, shortly thereafter, the fourth and final footbridge crosses another feeder creek. When the trail joins Ashley Road, you will have traveled 2.6 miles. Turn left onto the road, and keep an eye out for approaching traffic. Just across the river, you can turn right and walk into the parking lot for the San Juan mission.

The Mission San Juan Capistrano was originally established as San José de los Nazonis in east Texas. Relocated to this spot in 1731, it oversaw a rich agricultural area and orchards that supported not only the mission but the nearby settlements and presidio. Take the time to explore the old building before heading back up the trail to the Mission San José.

NORTH OF SAN ANTONIO

53   BAR-O RANCH LOOP

KEY AT-A-GLANCE INFORMATION

LENGTH: 4.4 miles

CONFIGURATION: Loop

DIFFICULTY: Moderate

SCENERY: Wide creek valley, cedar woods

EXPOSURE: Mostly open

TRAFFIC: Moderate

TRAIL SURFACE: Dirt, rocks

HIKING TIME: 2.75 hours

ACCESS: $6/person park-entrance fee

MAPS: At park headquarters or online at www.tpwd.state.tx.us/spdest/findadest/parks/hill_country

FACILITIES: Untreated water, privy at park headquarters

IN BRIEF

This hike travels the lower West Verde Creek Valley at Hill Country State Natural Area. Start at the park headquarters and make a wide loop around the old Bar-O Ranch. Along the way you'll see waterfalls, hillside cedar forests, old pastureland, and the valley of West Verde Creek.

DESCRIPTION

This hike traverses the lower elevations of Hill Country State Natural Area, staying in the vicinity of the old Bar-O Ranch main house. The main ranch house was built in 1916 and is used today by the Hill Country State Natural Area park manager. This is cattle country, and you will see relics from the ranch days. This hike through ranching history is in an appealing natural setting. You'll come to a small falls shortly after the trailhead, then climb into a hillside cedar forest, where the views open. Dip back down to West Verde Creek, where you'll pass the old Chapa House before ascending along West Verde Creek. Comanche Bluffs towers over the stream, which makes another drop at Chaquita Falls.

Park near the mailbox at park headquarters, then walk down the park road north, away from the mailbox and past the park office. Look

----

Directions

From San Antonio, take TX 16 to Bandera. In Bandera, turn left on TX 173 south, following it for one mile to FR 1077. Turn right onto FR 1077 and follow it for 10 miles to the park, where the road turns to dirt. Turn right into the park, crossing West Verde Creek, then turn right into the parking area near the park headquarters.

173
16 Bandera
To San Antonio
16
53
173
FR 1077
HILL COUNTRY STATE NATURAL AREA
N

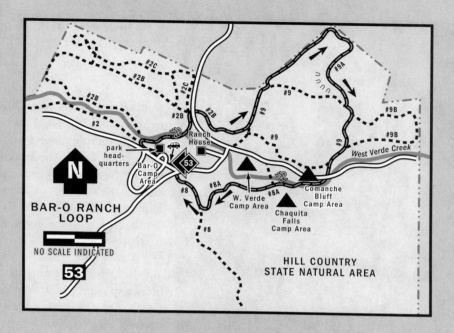

right for Trail #2, Bar-O Pasture Trail. Take Trail #2 and follow it just a bit before it splits. Stay to the right, passing through a fence, then keep along a fenceline to reach another junction. Trail #2B leaves left. Stay right, heading downstream along West Verde Creek, and pass a dam on the creek. You are heading toward the old two-story ranch house. At almost 0.5 miles, the trail crosses West Verde Creek just before reaching the house. Falls drop both above and below the crossing. The low flow of West Verde Creek makes the cascades less spectacular than they would be in more high-precipitation locations.

Pass an old barn, then reach an intersection at just over 0.5 miles. Trail #2C keeps forward. Trail #2B goes left and right. Turn right on Trail #2B to cross the county road heading toward Bandera. Immediately ascend a cedar-studded hill. The hills across West Verde Creek stand tall in the distance. The path is rocky in places. More good views open as you descend to reach a metal barn and Trail #9, Pasture Loop Trail. Veer left here onto a double-track path to cross a fence at 1.3 miles. Turn left here onto Trail #9A, Cedar Trail. Begin shadowing the cedar post and wire fence marking the park boundary. Ride the fenceline like an old Texas cowpoke checking for breaches. The narrow path curves with the boundary fence ahead and enters dense woods near the dam of an old pond.

The trail opens up to a hillside beyond the dam. Hill Country State Natural Area stands before you to the west. At 2.6 miles, intersect Trail #9. Keep right here, heading downhill. In a short distance Trail #9B, Eagle Trail, leaves left. This

is a good side trip if you want to extend the loop. Dip to cross another pond dam and reach fertile ground that is an open field. The back-side of the Chapa House lies ahead. Reach the Chapa House at 3.2 miles. This is another part of the former ranch complex.

Cross the park road and head for the low-water bridge spanning West Verde Creek. Directly beside West Verde Creek is Trail #8A, Chaquita Falls Trail. Head upstream along West Verde Creek on Chaquita Falls Trail. The two deep pools are popular fishing and swimming holes. The Comanche Bluff Camping Area is just to the right of the trail. The actual Comanche Bluffs are to the left of the stream. Cross the stream ahead at 3.4 miles. A simple rock hop is in order, except for during floods, when you wouldn't be on the trail at all. Enter a live oak cathedral before emerging just above Chaquita Falls. This wide, low-flow water feature slips over a rock slab into a pool. The Chaquita Falls Camp Area is nearby on this side of the stream.

A mix of grass and trees lies ahead backed by a tall bluff. At 4.1 miles, intersect the Hightower Trail. Turn right here and cruise through mixed woods and open country to reach the park headquarters trailhead.

CIBOLO NATURE CENTER HIKE 54

IN BRIEF

This is a wonderful area and an easy hike where families can learn about the various ecosystems represented in the preserve, located on the outskirts of Boerne. A wetland boardwalk, tall grass prairie, and dinosaur tracks will hold the interest of even the youngest hikers.

DESCRIPTION

Nestled on the east side of Boerne, just 22 miles northwest of San Antonio, the 100-acre Cibolo Nature Center attracts thousands of visitors each year. This nature preserve and environmental learning center contain numerous exhibits that educate hikers and visitors about the area's distinct ecosystems. Inside the visitor center are any number of informative pamphlets, including lists of birds typically found in the area as well as some nature books on Texas.

The trailhead is located at a pavilion north of the visitor center, where you will also find restrooms. The three plaques here display a map of the trail system, give information on the ecological areas, and explain the dinosaur tracks located 80 feet up the trail.

Continue past the plaques to reach the tracks, which are actually replicas of prints uncovered at the Boerne Lake spillway in June 1997 after a flood. The spillway is inaccessible to the public, so Peggy Maceo, an Austin-area artist, made these exact copies to be placed

KEY AT-A-GLANCE INFORMATION

LENGTH: 2.9 miles

CONFIGURATION: Irregular

DIFFICULTY: Easy

SCENERY: Wetlands, tall grass, Cibolo Creek, and surrounding woodlands

EXPOSURE: Very sunny–very shady

TRAFFIC: Moderate

TRAIL SURFACE: Grass, dirt, and boardwalk

HIKING TIME: 1.5 hours

ACCESS: Open 8 a.m.–6 p.m. No fees, but donations welcome

MAPS: Trail maps available in the visitor center

FACILITIES: Restrooms and picnic tables; beverages and gifts available in the visitor center

SPECIAL COMMENTS: For further information, contact the Cibolo Nature Center at (830) 249-4616 or online at www.cibolo.org

----

Directions ———————————→

From Exit 542 on Interstate 10, take US 87 to Boerne. From Boerne, take TX 46 east toward Boerne City Park; turn right on City Park Road. Cibolo Nature Center is on the right and is marked by a sign at its gate.

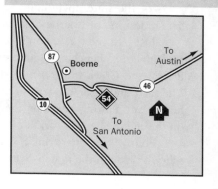

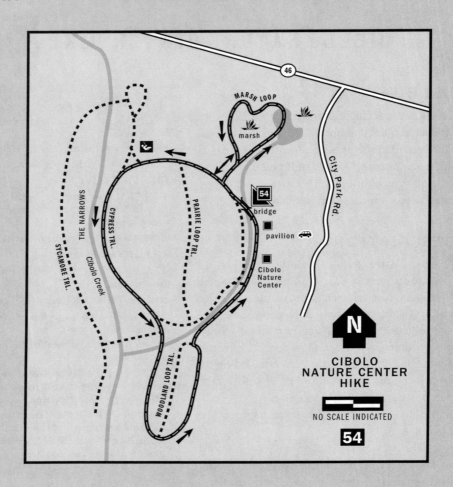

CIBOLO
NATURE CENTER
HIKE

NO SCALE INDICATED

54

here for public view. Molds were made of the original prints and then cast in concrete and arranged to replicate the spillway site. The dinosaur that made these prints is identified as the carnivore *Acrocanthosaurus* and has been found in other parts of the state, including the famous Glenn Rose formation in central Texas. The limestone of Boerne Lake is part of this same formation.

Just past the tracks you'll reach a wooden bridge spanning a creek bed, then a trail junction, bench, and accompanying directional signs. You'll head left to the Prairie and Creek trails in a bit, but meanwhile head right along the Marsh Loop. The surrounding area is part of the replicated tall-grass prairie, with numerous birdhouses and nesting boxes on the property. Look closely and you'll see a bat house on the right. The trail forks at 0.2 miles. Stay right and return from the left.

Follow the boardwalk, which was built by students from the local high school, through the marsh. Set on short pilings, the walkway carries you right into the middle of the marsh for an up-close look. A short distance ahead the board-walk expands into a wider deck area, where a bench is set up overlooking the largest part of the pool. The water here is crystal clear. Small fish and insects swim on and below its surface. The marsh area is also home to several bird species, including cattle egret, redwing blackbirds, and kingfishers. A smaller deck amidst the tall grass lies just beyond this point.

The boardwalk ends at the edge of the Boerne City Park. The trail turns to the left and loops back into the preserve, along the edge of the marsh. Another bench on the trail allows you to observe the marsh from outside of it. Just beyond this, the loop closes and the trail returns to the junction, where you'll see a marker designating the area as the Hilmar-Bergman Historical Prairie. This time follow the directional signs to the Prairie Loop Trail. Just before you reach a playground area and covered kiosk, you'll come to a trail intersection to the left. Take this trail to hike down toward the creek. The path soon crosses a dirt road where a sign warns drivers of hikers in the area. Cross the road and continue down the trail.

The trail joins Cibolo Creek, marked on the trail map as The Narrows. As you walk beside the creek, you'll notice how clear the water is. The creek area is part of the Texas Watch Stream Monitoring program and is checked for quality regularly as a critical source of recharge for the Edwards Aquifer. Anglers are occasionally seen here hoping to hook into one of the creek's bass or catfish that can easily be seen from some of the higher points on the trail. Snapping turtles also make their homes here.

The tall cypress trees provide ample shade for this part of the hike, which narrows considerably. After walking about 0.2 miles into the Cypress Trail, you'll encounter an earthen staircase leading away from the creek. Take these stairs, which will join you with the Woodland Loop Trail. Turn right onto the trail.

The environment here could not differ more from the tall grass prairie you walked through earlier. Oaks and junipers create a dense canopy over this trail, which follows the creek bluff before looping back north. Deer, rabbits, and numerous birds make their home in the cover provided by the trees, and the American beautybush and Mexican buckeye stay on the ground. Keep an ear open for rustling in the brush, and you might catch a glimpse of the nine-banded armadillo.

As the trail winds through the woodlands, it meets with a high electric fence 1.2 miles into the hike. This fence serves to keep predators out of the ranch across it. A bench faces the fence, offering views of birds and wildlife on the other side.

Not far past the bench, the path splits. Take the trail to the left, which leads back to the creek.

You'll soon return to the earthen stairs leading back down to the creek. Walk down and turn right to backtrack toward the kiosk area and the remainder of the Prairie Loop. When you reach the road you crossed before (1.8 miles), turn left onto it and hike past the picnic tables to your left. This section is the Cypress Trail on the map.

Continue hiking along the river until you reach the edge of the city park's soccer fields at 2.3 miles. Turn to the right. Numerous trees here are protected by fencing, and the map designates the area as the Tree of Life Arboretum. At nearly 2.5 miles, you'll see tennis courts on your left. Directly to your right is the beginning of another trail. This leads through the grassland prairie and back to the visitor center. Take this trail. As you walk along with the tall grass on both sides, look and listen for rattlesnakes and rabbits coming in and out of the thick prairie. At 2.8 miles, the trail rejoins the Prairie Loop Trail, which lead left to the pavilion. Turn left here and head back that way, then take the right, which leads to the small wooden bridge and the visitor center, where you can stop in and visit with the staff, pick up something cold to drink, and maybe make a contribution to their ongoing project.

GUADALUPE HIKE 55

IN BRIEF

There are two ways to approach hiking in the Guadalupe River State Park: as a nature watcher or as a people watcher. The first half of the hike offers a great view of the Guadalupe River; at certain times of year, it also provides a good view of people's picnics. The second half offers a secluded feeling as you work your way to a great viewing point.

DESCRIPTION

A popular spot for all types of outdoor enthusiasts, the Guadalupe River State Park has managed to maintain its rugged beauty in spite of the large number of visitors that it receives. Located on a 9-mile stretch of the Guadalupe River, the park includes 4 miles of river frontage, multiple campsites, and day-use areas. During the summer months it is almost sure to be full to capacity because of the cold waters of the river. The best times to visit during this season would be early in the week and as early in the morning as possible. The sounds of frolickers and the smells of picnics can be distracting during an otherwise serene hike.

The first half of this hike is more of a primitive road than an improved trail. It follows the riverfront and offers incredible views

KEY AT-A-GLANCE INFORMATION

LENGTH: 2 miles for riverfront, 1 mile for loop

CONFIGURATION: Balloon

DIFFICULTY: Moderate

SCENERY: Limestone cliffs, picnic areas, live-oak grassland

EXPOSURE: Shaded—open

TRAFFIC: Heavy on some parts of trail, very light on others

TRAIL SURFACE: Mostly packed gravel, some rocks

HIKING TIME: 1.5 hours for entire hike

ACCESS: Open to day use 8 a.m.– 10 p.m.; $3 entrance fee. Texas Conservation Passport holders are exempt from fees

MAPS: Available at the park office or online at www.tpwd.state.tx.us/ spdest/findadest/parks/guadalupe_ river

FACILITIES: Indoor toilets and showers in main parking area; chemical toilet at end of main trail; vending machines at main parking area

SPECIAL COMMENTS: This park is a popular warm-weather destination for swimmers. Early morning in the summer would be the best time to go, or any time of day during fall and early spring. River is subject to flash flooding during heavy rains. Contact park office at (830) 438-2656 for current conditions.

Directions

From Exit 189 on I-35 in New Braunfels, take TX 46 west for about 25 miles, and turn right (north) on Park Road 31, which ends in Guadalupe River State Park. Follow the park road until you reach the turnoff for the primitive campsites. Turn right and follow the road until it ends in a parking lot, less than 0.5 miles. The trailhead is clearly marked by a bulletin board sign with a map of the park and trails.

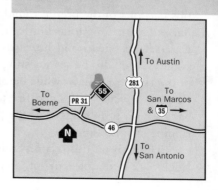

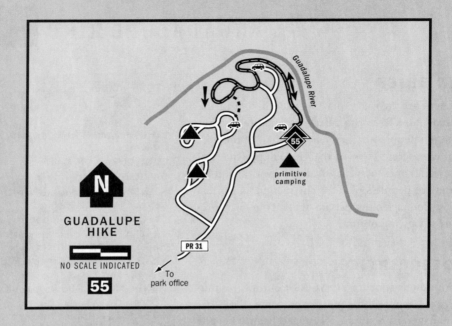

into the heart of the Texas Hill Country. Paddlers, anglers, bird-watchers, and hikers alike share this section of the park without getting in each other's way. There are numerous benches to rest on along the trail and, when the weather is favorable, a dip in the river will definitely serve to cool you off. If you are looking for a shorter hike, you may want to park in the more northern parking lot and just hike the loop.

Follow the trail as it winds down the ridge about 200 yards. This is the steepest slope you will encounter on the hike. The canopy of hardwoods at this point is home to a variety of birds, but the environment is more suited to listening to them than watching. When the trail reaches the river, you'll turn toward the left and begin hiking north along the banks of the Guadalupe. Rapids make this part one of the prettiest (and noisiest) parts of the river. The opposite side is flanked with limestone bluffs that have been eroded by centuries of flowing waters, and hawks and buzzards are constantly soaring along its edges. Small swallows can also be seen nesting in holes in the bluff. The trail follows the edge of the river for a short while before it separates from the bank, making room for numerous picnic tables and fire pits. During non-peak times, walking along the bank isn't a problem, but as the park gets busy, staying on the trail will prevent ruining anyone's picnic.

The trail on this section ends about the same way it began, winding up the ridge back into a parking lot, about a mile and a half from where you started. If you are in need of a break by this point, there is a full restroom with showers and vending machines in the parking area.

If you've had enough, turn around and return the way you came. Otherwise, walk across the lot toward the sign that points the way toward the amphitheater, and follow the designated trail. Here, the terrain varies greatly from the river-front into old-growth hardwoods. Cedar, live oaks, and elm provide shade and narrow the trail, which becomes more pressed dirt than gravel with pieces of limestone jutting from the ground. The map available from the park headquarters shows this trail as an out-and-back, but it is in fact a loop. Shortly into the trail, you'll reach a fork. You'll return on the left fork, so stay to the right for now. The forested area provides a respite from the sun along the riverbank, and the birds become a lot more vocal than visual. If you're attentive, you might catch a glimpse of an endangered golden-cheeked warbler, which nests in an area of the park. Along the trail the trees will thin to reveal something not often seen anymore— the live-oak grassland. These small to large openings are full of wildflowers and butterflies in the spring and are often frequented by whitetail deer year-round.

The incline of the trail gradually increases, reaching its peak underneath a huge cedar tree. There is a wooden bench strategically located here, and it's a great spot to sit, rest, and just reflect on the hike so far. The view from this point is breathtaking and includes treetops and valleys that make up the diverse ecosys-tem of the park. As you begin the hike back down the trail, look to the left. You'll see the roof and windmill of a long-abandoned residence amid the green of the trees. This is as good a place for a panoramic photo as you'll find in this part of the state. The trail eventually joins back up with itself; continue to the right to return to the parking lot. From this point, you can walk back along the river or follow the park road to see more of the grasslands and the wildlife that may be visible in it. Either way is roughly the same distance, and the road offers an easier walk without repeating the view from the first part of the hike. Just look for the sign designating the hike-in campsites and turn left. You'll find your car right where you left it.

56   GUADALUPE RIVER TRAIL

KEY AT-A-GLANCE INFORMATION

LENGTH: 1 mile

CONFIGURATION: Out-and-back

DIFFICULTY: Moderate

SCENERY: Lush woods and the Guadalupe River

EXPOSURE: Shady

TRAFFIC: Light

TRAIL SURFACE: Gravel, dirt, and roots

HIKING TIME: 30 minutes

ACCESS: Open to day use

MAPS: None

FACILITIES: None

IN BRIEF

Known to fly fishermen throughout the state as the premier spot for the long rod, this isolated trail located near the Canyon Lake Tailrace also offers hikers a quiet reprieve from the busier parks in the summer. Lush foliage creates an ideal spot for watching the river's visitors and inhabitants go about their business.

DESCRIPTION

The water from the Guadalupe River exits the Canyon Lake Dam just upstream from here and offers the coldest year-round water in the state. Anglers from all over the state know it as the only place where rainbow trout exist throughout the year, and it is a closely guarded secret. Just downriver a ways, inner tube, kayak, and canoe enthusiasts begin a traditional spring and summer float trip that can lead the hard-core floaters all the way to New Braunfels.

The river recreation here is commonly thought of as anything but tranquil. However, this well-hidden trail begins and ends before the sometimes rowdy floaters begin their trek. For birders, anglers, and nature watchers, it is a small oasis of tranquility located in one of the busiest summertime getaway spots in the state.

Directions

From I-35 South, take FM 306 west to South Access Road. Turn left on South Access Road and look on the left for the park entrance. There are two parking areas. Turn into the second parking lot. A large sign at the end designates the beginning of the trail.

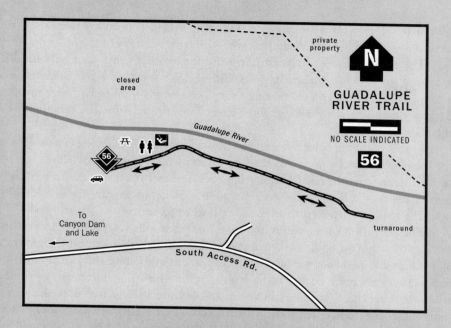

A short hike through the thick bottoms of the river, this trail offers birders a chance to see the endangered black-capped vireo playing in the tall tops of the trees. Another draw is the population of wading birds that one would normally observe on the lakes or near the coast. The shallow pools and eddies here create a natural environment for birds like sand pipers, egrets, and herons to probe for a meal or rest in the tranquility of this lush watershed.

The trail begins by descending a short earthen staircase at the end of the parking lot. There is a wooden bridge located almost immediately after the stairs, then a second one within 500 feet. The first half of the trail is very well kept, with wood guards keeping the gravel of the trail even and easy to traverse. The river is barely visible through the dense trees, but the sounds of the water are always present. The thick plants and wildflowers are natural attractants for a variety of butterflies in the spring and summer. The canopy and the cool air coming off the river keep this hike relatively cool throughout the year. Numerous spurs lead to the river, where it is generally shallow enough to wade. Anglers use these trails to get to prime fishing spots.

You'll encounter a bench and scenic river overlook 0.2 miles into the trail, where you can watch the wading birds and anglers play in the river. Even if you aren't an angler, the display put on by a skilled fly fisherman can be entrancing. The hypnotic rhythms used to deftly place the delicate lures within striking distance of hungry trout will entrance most observers, who quickly learn that the sport has more to do with casting than catching fish. It is an art form that one must observe to truly appreciate, and this is a great location to see it.

The trail continues at its current state for another tenth of a mile until it reaches a set of wood-and-earth stairs leading downward, where it narrows into a simple dirt path. If you're wearing shorts, you might want to consider turning back at this point. The thick ground cover hugs the trail for the remainder of the hike.

At this point the habitat becomes very inviting to black-capped vireos. Listen for their singing and scan the treetops for motion. The tiny, reclusive birds can be seen hanging from the branches, darting back and forth between the trees. You'll have to be very still and quiet to get a good look at this endangered bird. They offer their songs, however, to even the nosiest of passersby.

The attraction of the water and surrounding woods is irresistible to numerous small mammals. Squirrels are abundant both in the trees and on the ground, and nutria can be heard rummaging in the weeds and along the bank. Looking like a cross between a beaver and a big rat, the herbivorous nutria can be somewhat alarming the first time you see one. They are usually harmless and want nothing to do with people, so they'll insist you watch them from a distance. Most of the small holes you see along this and other river trails in the area are made by them rooting for food.

The trail continues to push into the thick woodland until you reach a point where you simply can't go any farther—a little more than 0.5 miles from the trailhead. Not far off the trail, there is a wetlands restoration habitat. This trail is under a constant state of improvement; hopefully it will someday connect with the wetlands viewing area. Maintained by the U.S. Army Corps of Engineers, both areas would make a great wild attraction in this otherwise busy area.

As you return, take the time to observe the damage floods can do the landscape. Numerous large trees lay on their sides, victims of raging floods.

HIGHTOWER TRAIL HIKE

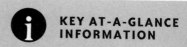

IN BRIEF

Hill Country State Natural Area is the setting for this fine loop. Work away from park headquarters up to high points with views. Circle around former ranch country before descending to West Verde Creek, where great views await at Comanche Bluff. Finally, pass an old ranch homestead, then follow the creek past Chaquita Falls, a small cascade on West Verde Creek.

DESCRIPTION

This is one of my favorite hikes in central Texas. It shows off the Hill Country at its finest, passing across both forested and open peaks where you can look out on wildlands. At the same time, it visits old ranch relics, for the Hill Country is ranch country if nothing else. The water feature of West Verde Creek adds contrast to the loop—you overlook the watercourse from Comanche Bluff before dropping creekside to view Chaquita Falls.

The Hightower Trail begins near the mailbox near the park headquarters. Trails at Hill Country State Natural Area are marked with numbered plastic posts. Leave the headquarters area on Trail #8, Hightower Trail. Shortly pass through a break in an old fence. At 0.3 miles, the Hightower Trail stays forward

KEY AT-A-GLANCE INFORMATION

LENGTH: 4.3 miles
CONFIGURATION: Loop
DIFFICULTY: Moderate–difficult
SCENERY: Wooded hills, creek
EXPOSURE: Partly shady
TRAFFIC: Moderate, busy on spring and fall weekends
TRAIL SURFACE: Rocks aplenty, dirt
HIKING TIME: 2.75 hours
ACCESS: $6/person park-entrance fee
MAPS: At park office or online at www.tpwd.state.tx.us/spdest/findadest/parks/hill_country
FACILITIES: Untreated water and privy near park office

Directions

From San Antonio, take TX 16 to Bandera. In Bandera, turn left on TX 173 south, following 173 for 1 mile to FR 1077. Turn right onto FR 1077 and follow it 10 miles to the park, where the road turns to dirt. Turn right in the park, crossing West Verde Creek, then turn right again into the park headquarters. Park near the headquarters or across the road near the Bar-O Ranch Camping Area.

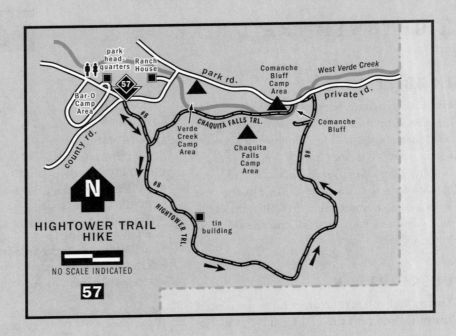

with a double-track path, whereas Trail #8A, the Chaquita Falls Trail, splits to the left. The Chaquita Falls Trail is part of your return route.

Begin to ascend a partly wooded hill. Views open to your west atop the hill. Live oaks grow plentifully up here. The Hightower Trail drifts through live oak groves. At almost 1 mile, the path bisects an old ranch gate near a tin shed. Cut through a second gate, and descend into a grassy swale before climbing toward a small transmission line. Turn left here to top a second hill. The trail is very rocky on the downgrade. Boulders, pebbles, and stones of every size cover the trail. Dip to an old watering hole at 1.7 miles. A concrete basin, shed, and salt lick are hereabouts.

The Hightower Trail now undulates northerly through hills. Views open up, and the solitude is palpable. No sounds of trucks rumbling in the distance here. Begin to follow a rocky wash before crossing it to make a gap in the ridgeline to your left. Descend from the gap toward West Verde Creek on a double-track path. Look for a side trail leading left at 2.7 miles. This trail, the Comanche Bluffs Trail, is easily missed. This path leads 0.1 mile left to bluffs overlooking West Verde Creek. The rock bluffs shadow the clear pools of the water course. Comanche Bluffs Camp Area is below in the grove of live oak trees. You can also see the low-water bridge downstream on the creek, which you will be crossing shortly.

Backtrack and resume descending to a private ranch road. Turn left here and cross the low-water bridge. The Chapa House is to the right of the bridge.

Overlooking West Verde Creek

The route turns left just after the low-water bridge, now as the Chaquita Falls Trail. Begin to cruise along West Verde Creek. Look for turtles sunning on logs and rocks, and for bream beneath the water. Comanche Bluff Camping Area is just to the right of the trail. Cross the stream ahead at 3.3 miles, a task that should be easy in times of normal flow. Stroll beneath live oaks before you climb out just above Chaquita Falls, a wide cascade that drops four or five feet into a pool. The Chaquita Falls Camp Area is nearby on this side of the stream.

A mix of grass and trees lies ahead. A tall bluff to the left is visible from open areas. To your right you can see the old Bar-O Ranch homesite, built in 1916. At 4 miles, you'll intersect the Hightower Trail. Turn right here and backtrack 0.3 miles to the trailhead.

NEARBY ACTIVITIES

Hill Country State Natural Area offers walk-in tent camping, backpacking, bicycling, horseback riding, and fishing. For more information, call (800) 792-1112 or visit **www.tpwd.state.tx.us/spdest/findadest/parks/hill_country**.

58 HILL COUNTRY CREEK AND CANYON TREK

KEY AT-A-GLANCE INFORMATION

LENGTH: 7.8 miles

CONFIGURATION: Loop

DIFFICULTY: Difficult

SCENERY: Wooded and open hills, canyons, creek bottomland

EXPOSURE: Mostly open

TRAFFIC: Moderate–potentially busy on nice spring and fall weekends

TRAIL SURFACE: Dirt, rocks

HIKING TIME: 5.5 hours

ACCESS: $6/person park-entrance fee

MAPS: At park office and online at www.tpwd.state.tx.us/spdest/findadest/parks/hill_country

FACILITIES: Untreated water spigot, privy, and park office

IN BRIEF

This challenging hike traverses the highs and lows of Hill Country State Natural Area. You'll begin along the creek bottoms of a wide valley, then climb into some bona fide Hill Country after a lung-buster climb. Dip down to a backcountry campsite before roaming into Cougar Canyon, where views await you. From here, a long downgrade eases the pain of the trek's end.

DESCRIPTION

This is one of the best hikes in the entire Hill Country region. It explores all the different environments Hill Country State Natural Area offers. Much of the hike offers a truly wild feel, and if you are up to the task, two back-pack campsites are on the way. Leave the main day-use trailhead at the end of public vehicular access, and begin to walk down the closed park road north, away from the park office, up the West Verde Creek Valley.

At 0.1 mile, turn right onto Trail #6, Spring Branch Trail. The trails at Hill Country State Natural Area are numbered on plastic posts in the field and have corresponding names. All trails in the park are open to hikers, bikers, and equestrians. Descend through broken woods and pasture to shortly meet Trail

----

Directions ⟶

From San Antonio, take TX 16 to Bandera. In Bandera, turn left on TX 173 south, following 173 for 1 mile to FR 1077. Turn right onto FR 1077 and follow it 10 miles to the park, where the road turns to dirt. Turn right into the park, crossing West Verde Creek, then turn right again, passing the park headquarters. Continue to the day-use parking area on your left.

173

16　　Bandera

N

16　　To San Antonio

58

FR 1077　　173

HILL COUNTRY STATE NATURAL AREA

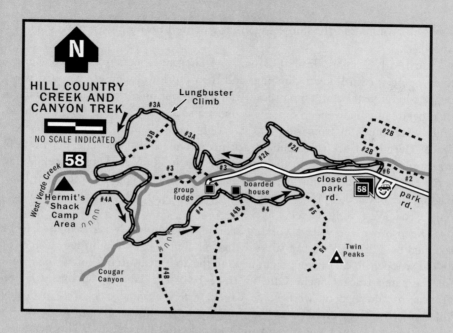

#2, Bar-O Pasture Trail, just on this side of West Verde Creek. Turn left here. West Verde Creek is on your right and the hills of Twin Peaks are to the left. Ahead, Trail #2B leaves right—keep forward to meet Trail #2A, Creek Bottom Trail, at 0.5 miles. Turn right here, immediately stepping over the streambed of West Verde Creek. Begin cruising thick woods bordering the park boundary fence. At just over a mile, a boundary fence gate leads right to a private equestrian lodge. Veer left here, looking for a quick right turn onto a single-track path. Do not stay forward on the wide roadbed—you will end at the closed park road. The single-track path, the correct trail, goes over a small berm and beside an old pond bed to the right before entering dense and appealing woods.

Ahead, the woods open a bit—songbirds accompany the deep green hue of the juniper, contrasting with the brown grass at your feet and the brilliant blue Texas sky overhead. At nearly 2 miles, in a live oak thicket, pick up Trail #3, Hermit's Trace. Begin to climb and remember to look back for good views to the south and west. Climb over a couple of deep washes to reach a trail junction at about 2.5 miles. Turn right here, picking up Trail #3A, Good Luck Trail. This is named for the luck you'll need in surmounting its steep ups and downs. Immediately start your first ascent. Gravity will prove that you are really in Texas Hill Country. The junipers offer enough space between them to allow views all around and the knowledge that you are heading into a bowl encircled by ridges.

At nearly 3 miles, Trail #3B (with no alternative name) leaves to the left. Keep going forward, keep climbing, and then dip into a densely wooded wash. Begin a lung-buster climb on a rocky trail to top out on a ridge. Gather yourself, then begin an equally steep descent to meet a rock wash at mile 3.4. Just ahead, Trail #3B comes in from the left, stay right here to meet Trail #3, Hermit's Trace. Hermit's Trace is a double-track path. This is an important junction. To your right 0.3 miles away, in the uppermost reaches of West Verde Creek Valley, is the Hermit's Shack Camp Area for equestrians and backpackers. Turn left here, passing the Butterfly Springs Camp Area on your right, which is for backpackers only. Cross West Verde Creek.

Keep down the valley, working around a wide-open wash that used to be spanned by a bridge. You can still see the soil abutment of the bridge. Watch for an old wooden shack on your right beyond the abutment. At 4.2 miles, look right for the single-track Cougar Canyon Trail, Trail #4. Take the Cougar Canyon Trail across the bed of West Verde Creek, where skeletal oaks were probably killed in a fire from times past. The Panther Canyon draw is to your left. At 4.5 miles, Trail #4A, the Cougar Canyon Overlook Trail, leaves right. This dead-end path heads a half-mile to the hill above and a far-reaching vista (total hike mileage does not include this side trip).

The Cougar Canyon Trail crosses Cougar Canyon on an old pond dam, then dips to a small wash before ascending the ridge dead ahead. Top out on the ridge, where Trail #4B (with no other name) leaves to the right. You will likely notice the view ahead more than the trail leaving right. Here, the West Verde Valley stretches far in the distance, far to the east. Begin working down the valley in broken juniper woodland, passing an old tin shack in the next wash, which is wooded with live oak. Come along a fence line. Ahead, you can see the park group lodge.

At 5.8 miles, pass through a gate. Trail #4 goes both ways. Turn right here and soon come to a boarded house on your left. At the house, Trail #4B goes right. Stay left on Hermit's Trace and cross the dam of an old pond. Reach another trail junction in moist woods at 6.3 miles. Turn left here onto Trail #5, Twin Peaks Trail. Dip through shady oaks and other hardwoods before briefly opening into juniper. Return to lush woods with many a tall tree along a flat by West Verde Creek. Sycamores line the banks of the streambed. Shortly, you'll reach the park road, which is closed to private vehicular traffic, near a culvert. Turn right here and walk a short distance before veering left onto Trail #2, Bar-O Pasture Trail. The grass and soil footing and the wide-open valley bottom contrast greatly with the rocky hills through which you've been traveling.

Keep in grassland through the heart of the valley. At 7.3 miles, intersect Trail #2A, Creek Bottom Trail. This completes the loop portion of the trek. Keep forward on Trail #2, backtracking to Trail #6, and return to the trailhead.

NEARBY ACTIVITIES

Hill Country State Natural Area offers walk-in tent camping, backpacking, bicycling, horseback riding, and fishing. For more information, call (800) 792-1112 or visit **www.tpwd.state.tx.us/spdest/findadest/parks/hill_country.**

59 KERRVILLE-SCHREINER PARK LOOP

KEY AT-A-GLANCE INFORMATION

LENGTH: 3.5 miles
CONFIGURATION: Loop
DIFFICULTY: Moderate
SCENERY: Hill Country woods
EXPOSURE: Mostly open
TRAFFIC: Moderate
TRAIL SURFACE: Gravel, rock, dirt
HIKING TIME: 2.5 hours
ACCESS: $4 per person park-entrance fee or $10 for 4–5 people in a vehicle; day-use access to park ends at 10 p.m.
MAPS: At park office or online at www.kerrville.org/index.asp?nid=318
FACILITIES: Water, restrooms at nearby campground

IN BRIEF

This loop hike encompasses several trails at this park just outside Kerrville. Ramble through juniper woods, topping out at a high point where you can overlook the Guadalupe River Valley below. Circle back off the hilltop to complete the loop. The many different trails here offer other loop combinations for hikers and mountain bikers.

DESCRIPTION

The trails here at Kerrville-Schreiner Park are color coded. You will be traveling a series of these paths to make a loop. A park map is a definite help in making this route, but it is not so complicated as this narrative implies when you are in the field with map in hand. So don't get so caught up in staying on the correct trail that you miss out on all the scenery!

Leave Trailhead #3, and immediately enter a shady juniper forest on the Yellow Trail. Plastic posts indicating the trail have been placed at trail intersections. A color-coded

Directions

From San Antonio, head north on I-10 to Exit 508, TX 16. Take TX 16 south and travel 0.3 miles to east Loop Road 534. Turn left on Loop Road 534. Keep forward on Loop 534, crossing the Guadalupe River, and reach TX 173 at 4.3 miles. Turn left on TX 173, and then turn left at 0.1 mile to enter Kerrville-Schreiner Park. The park headquarters is in the center of the entrance island just as you enter the park. Stop at the park headquarters to obtain entrance permits, gate codes, and park maps. After your stop, continue on to reach the trailhead. Head toward the camping area; Trailhead #3 will be on your left just beyond the right turn into the park group shelter.

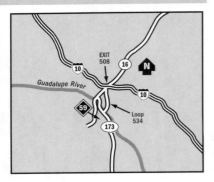

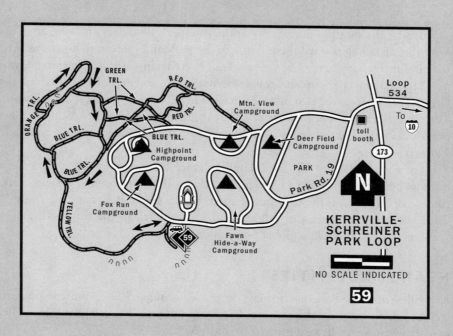

band with an accompanying arrow is atop the plastic post. Occasional oaks and grass vary the woodland. At 0.1 mile, the pea-gravel portion of the path, an all-access trail, splits left and goes to an overlook beyond the park boundary. Keep forward on the Yellow Trail, coming alongside a rock shelf to the left. The trail opens to a fenceline marking the park border. Here, you can enjoy views of the hills, cattle country, and creeping suburbanization.

The forest opens. Look for narrow deer paths crisscrossing the trail. At almost 1 mile, veer left onto the Blue Trail, staying with it for nearly 0.5 miles, and pick up the Orange Trail. Stay left on a narrower path, ascending to reach another junction at almost 1.5 miles. Stay left again as the Orange Trail splits. Begin to climb steadily on a rooty track, and gain the hilltop just below a water tower. Here, you can look through the juniper trees onto the Guadalupe Valley below.

The Guadalupe River flowing through the Hill Country originally attracted Native Americans, who lived in the area off and on for 10,000 years; white settlers came in the early 1800s. The town of Kerrville was perched on a bluff near the river. Originally a shinglemaker's camp named Brownsborough, it became Kerrville in the 1850s. But it wasn't until a pair of German settlers built a mill here that the town began to grow. This growth spawned Charles A. Schreiner's multifaceted businesses, which in turn spurred the further growth of Kerrville. Schreiner shares the name of the park near the town he helped develop.

Descend along the fenceline marking the park boundary, making an acute right turn, heading toward the interior of the park and more trail junctions. The path is mostly shady here. The Orange Trail splits again—stay left, keeping downhill. The country opens up and grasses become more common. Now, intersect the Green Trail at just over two miles. Stay right here, dipping through a small wash. The Green Trail goes both ways at the next junction—stay right. All these junctions are a pain, but this loop is attempting to cover the most scenic ground and still make sense.

Intersect the Blue Trail at 2.3 miles. Turn left here and follow it a short distance before it splits. Turn right, leaving the roadbed and joining a rocky track. Ahead, at 2.7 miles, is the final intersection. It may seem oddly familiar, and it is. Turn left here, rejoining the Yellow Trail to backtrack to the trailhead, maybe wishing you had brought a global positioning system.

NEARBY ACTIVITIES

Kerrville-Schreiner Park has fishing on the Guadalupe River, and camping, as well as hiking and mountain biking. For more information, call (830) 257-5392 or visit **www.kerrville.org/index.asp?nid=318.**

TWIN PEAKS TRAIL 60

IN BRIEF

This rugged hike up a central Texas hill to one of the best views around for miles is followed up with a stroll down to the valley you were viewing from the peak.

DESCRIPTION

The Hill Country State Natural Area is as rugged as a park can get and still attract visitors. A haven for horse lovers, mountain bikers, and hikers alike, this park was designed solely for their use. Deeded to the Texas Parks and Wildlife Department under conditions that it is kept as wild and natural as possible, this area has had little done in the way of improvements. There is no water or electricity to be had at the park, so unless campers bring a generator, they are limited to roughing it. Even with such conditions, campers should make reservations, as there are only ten campsites in the park.

The only other improvements made here are the marked trails (more than 40 miles' worth) and the horse stables in both the day-use and campsite areas. Hikers, riders, and bikers alike are allowed to use all the trails in the park, and rules of the road have been established to ensure peaceful cohabitation. While on the trails, bikers yield to hikers and horses, and hikers yield to horses. This is to

KEY AT-A-GLANCE INFORMATION

LENGTH: 3 miles
CONFIGURATION: Loop
DIFFICULTY: Moderate
SCENERY: Typical Hill Country vegetation ranging from mountain cedar to Spanish dagger (yucca), horseback riders and mountain bikers
EXPOSURE: Open
TRAFFIC: Moderate–heavy
TRAIL SURFACE: Dirt and rock, some loose gravel
HIKING TIME: 1.5 hours
ACCESS: Open for day use and limited camping; $6/person entry fee (TCP holders are exempt)
MAPS: Trail map available from park office
FACILITIES: Outhouses; water is not available here.

Directions

Take TX 16 West from San Antonio to Bandera. In Bandera, turn left on TX 173 South, and then right on FM 1077 1 mile past the junction. The road ends in the park after 10 miles, when it turns to dirt. Signs point you to turn right to reach the park headquarters. A ranger will point you to the trailhead parking area.

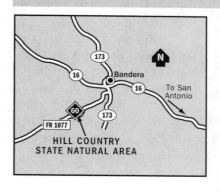

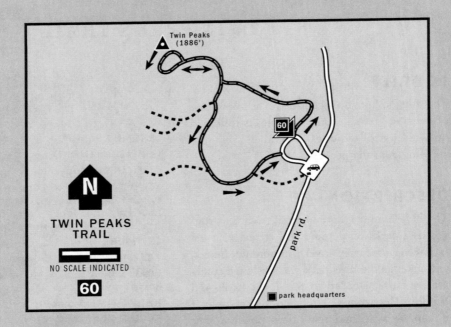

keep horses from getting spooked and hurting their riders, hikers, or themselves, and these rules are enforced with citations by the rangers, who are also law-enforcement officers. They will also cite visitors for straying off the trails. Do not go cross-country during your hikes here.

The park office is a simple portable building with a bulletin board. When you're checking in, the rangers will be happy to show the various highlights of the trails on the map, as well as to explain the symbols used to denote hazardous areas. Scenic areas are also marked, and the map is much more detailed than most state park maps. This park is for trailblazers. The trailhead is located in the camping areas west of the office. Park there and head to the trailhead between campsites 214 and 215, located about 0.1 mile from the parking spaces. Do not park in the campsites.

The trails in the park are numbered and marked with signs at intersections and points along the trails. Follow the trail from the campsites into the brush toward two obvious hills that almost appear to be connected. The trail is narrow and made of dirt at this point, and gradually climbs from the camping area. You'll reach a T-intersection 0.3 miles into the trail. Continue to the left to make your way to the two hills. From here the view already gets breathtaking. To your left you can see a good deal of the park, as you've climbed more than 100 feet above the parking area.

The trail intersects Trail 6 0.5 miles from the trailhead. You will turn here later. For now, remain on the trail you're on, which will fork 0.1 mile from the intersection. Continue to the left toward the peak and the view that awaits there. From this point on, the trail becomes loose gravel and can be tricky. A section of the trail is fashioned into crude steps using telephone-type poles and the gravel. Don't let this slight improvement cause you to let your guard down. Watch your step. This is one of the areas on the map marked as treacherous. The peak is located another 0.2 miles up the trail. From an elevation of 1,886 feet, you can look east, which reveals the camping area you just hiked through. From the rest of the peak you can view the rolling hills and cedars that make up this area of Texas. At just about any given time of day, you should be able to see horseback riders along the many trails visible from this point. You can easily imagine yourself in the Texas of 150 years ago.

As you come back down the hill the way you came, you'll return to the intersection with Trail 6. Take this fork to the right and meander through the valley you were just appreciating. The narrow trail wanders through cedar, live oak, and mesquite that are never really high enough to provide adequate shade. Attentive hikers have a good chance to catch sight of deer walking along the trail, stopping to browse on the numerous plants and herbs.

The trail continues for 0.8 miles, at which point it intersects Trail 1. Turn left onto this new trail that will lead you back to your vehicle. The path here is wide enough for vehicular traffic (which is not allowed) and shows obvious signs of use by both bikers and horseback riders. The trail almost sets a leisurely pace for you on the wide path, reminiscent of an old country road. It narrows to single-hiker width a half mile from the last intersection but quickly widens again afterward.

At 2.7 miles into your hike, you'll reach another fork that leads off Trail 5A. Stay on your present course, which will emerge in the campground 0.2 miles from the fork between campsites 215 and 216. Turn right here and head back to your car for fresh water before tackling one of the park's many other trails.

APPENDIXES AND INDEX

APPENDIX A:
HIKING STORES

AUSTIN

REI
9901 North Capital of Texas
   Highway, Suite 200
(512) 343-5550
601 North Lamar Boulevard
(512) 482-3357
www.rei.com

Whole Earth Provision Company
1014 North Lamar Boulevard
(512) 476-1414
4477 South Lamar Boulevard,
   Suite 200
(512) 899-0992
www.wholeearthprovision.com

SAN ANTONIO

Academy Sporting Goods
165 Southwest Military Drive
(210) 334-6740
2727 Northeast Loop 410
(210) 871-2630
www.academy.com

National Outdoors
5600 Bandera Road
(210) 680-3322
6900 San Pedro Avenue
(210) 979-8111

Sports Authority
125 Northwest Loop 410,
   Suite 140
(210) 341-1244
www.sportsauthority.com

Whole Earth Provision Company
255 East Basse Road, Suite 510
(210) 829-8888
www.wholeearthprovision.com

APPENDIX B:
PLACES TO BUY MAPS

AUSTIN

Mapsco Map & Travel Center
6406 North IH-35, Suite 1301
(888) 674-6277
(512) 302-9036
www.mapsco.com

Whole Earth Provision Company
1014 North Lamar Boulevard
(512) 476-1414
4477 South Lamar Boulevard,
   Suite 200
(512) 899-0992
www.wholeearthprovision.com

SAN ANTONIO

Mapsco Map & Travel Center
610 West Sunset Road
(800) 798-2112
(210) 829-7629
www.mapsco.com

Whole Earth Provision Company
255 East Basse Road, Suite 510
(210) 829-8888
www.wholeearthprovision.com

Alamo Group of the Sierra Club
P.O. Box 6443
San Antonio, TX 78209
texas.sierraclub.org/alamo

**Austin Regional Group of the
  Sierra Club**
P.O. Box 4581
Austin, TX 78765-5392
texas.sierraclub.org/austin

Central Texas Trail Tamers
P.O. Box 12045
Austin, TX 78711-2045
(512) 394-9998
www.trailtamers.org

Colorado River Walkers
(512) 281-0741
www.coloradoriverwalkers.org

Hill Country Outdoors
P.O. Box 684732
Austin, TX 78768-4732
(512) 383-1191
www.hillcountryoutdoors.com

INDEX

GPS OUTDOORS

by Russell Helms
ISBN 10: 0-89732-967-8
ISBN 13: 978-0-89732-967-5
$10.95
120pages

Whether you're a hiker on a weekend trip through the Great Smokies, a backpacker cruising the Continental Divide Trail, a mountain biker kicking up dust in Moab, a paddler running the Lewis and Clark bicentennial route, or a climber pre-scouting the routes up Mount Shasta, a simple handheld GPS unit is fun, useful, and can even be a lifesaver.

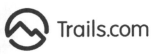

DEAR CUSTOMERS AND FRIENDS,

SUPPORTING YOUR INTEREST IN OUTDOOR ADVENTURE, travel, and an active lifestyle is central to our operations, from the authors we choose to the locations we detail to the way we design our books. Menasha Ridge Press was incorporated in 1982 by a group of veteran outdoorsmen and professional outfitters. For 25 years now, we've specialized in creating books that benefit the outdoors enthusiast.

Almost immediately, Menasha Ridge Press earned a reputation for revolutionizing outdoors- and travel-guidebook publishing. For such activities as canoeing, kayaking, hiking, backpacking, and mountain biking, we established new standards of quality that transformed the whole genre, resulting in outdoor-recreation guides of great sophistication and solid content. Menasha Ridge continues to be outdoor publishing's greatest innovator.

The folks at Menasha Ridge Press are as at home on a white-water river or mountain trail as they are editing a manuscript. The books we build for you are the best they can be, because we're responding to your needs. Plus, we use and depend on them ourselves.

We look forward to seeing you on the river or the trail. If you'd like to contact us directly, join in at **www.trekalong.com** or visit us at **www.menasharidge.com**. We thank you for your interest in our books and the natural world around us all.

SAFE TRAVELS,

Bob Sehlinger

BOB SEHLINGER
PUBLISHER